Śakti Sādhanā

Steps to Samādhi

ALSO BY PANDIT RAJMANA TIGUNAIT, PhD

BOOKS:

The Pursuit of Power and Freedom: Katha Upanishad
Touched by Fire: The Ongoing Journey of a Spiritual Seeker
Lighting the Flame of Compassion
Inner Quest: Yoga's Answers to Life's Questions
The Himalayan Masters: A Living Tradition
Why We Fight: Practices for Lasting Peace
At the Eleventh Hour: The Biography of Swami Rama
Swami Rama of the Himalayas: His Life and Mission
Tantra Unveiled: Seducing the Forces of Matter and Spirit
Shakti: The Power in Tantra (A Scholarly Approach)
From Death to Birth: Understanding Karma and Reincarnation
The Power of Mantra and the Mystery of Initiation
Shakti Sadhana: Steps to Samadhi
(A Translation of the Tripura Rahasya)
Seven Systems of Indian Philosophy

AUDIO & VIDEO:

Sacred Link™ Freedom from Fear Conference
The Quest for Freedom and the Sacred Link™
The Spirit of the Vedas
The Spirit of the Upanishads
Pulsation of the Maha Kumbha Mela
In the Footsteps of the Sages
Living Tantra™ Series
- *Tantric Traditions and Techniques*
- *The Secret of Tantric Rituals*
- *Forbidden Tantra*
- *Tantra and Kundalini*
- *Sri Chakra: The Highest Tantric Practice*
- *Sri Vidya: The Embodiment of Tantra*

ŚAKTI SĀDHANĀ
Steps to Samādhi

A Translation of the Tripurā Rahasya

by Pandit Rajmani Tigunait, PhD

with an Introduction by Swami Rama

HIMALAYAN INSTITUTE®
PRESS

Himalayan Institute Press
952 Bethany Turnpike
Honesdale, PA 18431

www.HimalayanInstitute.org

Second Printing 2008

Printed in the United States of America

ISBN-13: 978-0-89389-140-4
ISBN-10: 0-89389-140-1

LCCN: 93045897

SFI CERTIFIED SOURCING
FIBER USED IN THIS PRODUCT LINE MEETS THE SOURCING REQUIREMENTS OF THE SFI PROGRAM
WWW.SFIPROGRAM.ORG

Dedicated to The Mother alone

CONTENTS

The SPELLING and PRONUNCIATION of SANSKRIT LETTERS and WORDS

Sanskrit vowels are generally the same pure vowel sounds found in Italian, Spanish, or French. The consonants are generally pronounced as in English.

a	org*a*n, s*u*m
ā	f*a*ther
ai	*ai*sle
au	s*au*erkr*au*t
b	*b*ut
bh	a*bh*or
c	*ch*ur*ch*
ḍ	*d*ough
d	*d*ough (slightly toward the *th* sound of *th*ough)
ḍh	a*dh*ere
dh	a*dh*ere (slightly toward the *theh* sound of brea*the h*ere)
e	pr*ey*
g	*g*o
gh	do*gh*ouse
ḥ	[slight aspiration of preceding vowel]
h	*h*ot
i	*i*t
ī	pol*i*ce
j	*j*ump

jh	lo*dgeh*ouse
k	*k*id
kh	wor*kh*orse
l	*l*ug
ṃ or ṁ	[resonant nasalization of preceding vowel]
m	*m*ud
ṅ	si*ng*
ṇ	u*n*der
ñ	pi*ñ*ata
n	*n*o
o	n*o*
p	*p*ub
ph	u*ph*ill
ṛ	no English equivalent; a simple vowel *r*, such as appears in many Slavonic languages
r	*r*um
ś	*sh*awl (pronounced with a slight whistle; German *s*prechen)
ṣ	*sh*un
s	*s*un
ṭ	*t*omato
t	wa*t*er
ṭh	*Th*ailand
u	p*u*sh
ū	r*u*de
v	*v*odka (midway between *w* and *v*)
y	*y*es

Vowels. Every vowel is either long or short. The diphthongs *e, o, ai,* and *au* are always long. Long *a, i,* and *u* are indicated by a horizontal line over the vowel. The long form of a vowel is pronounced twice as long as the short form.

Consonants. Sanskrit has many aspirated consonants, that is, consonants pronounced with a slight *h* sound: *bh ch ḍh dh gh jh kh ph ṭh th.* These apirated consonants should be pronounced distinctly. The retroflex consonants, *ḍ ḍh ṇ ṣ ṭ ṭh,* are pronounced with a hitting sound, as the tip of the tongue is curled back to the ridge of the hard palate. The dentals, *d dh n t th,* are pronounced with the tip of the tongue touching the upper teeth.

Accentuation. There is no strong accentuation of syllables. The general rule is to stress the next-to-last syllable of a word, if that is long. A syllable is long if (*a*) it has a long vowel or (*b*) its vowel is followed by more than one consonant. If the next-to-last syllable of a word is short, then the syllable before that receives the stress.

INTRODUCTION
by Swami Rama

ALL HUMAN BEINGS EXPERIENCE the waking, dreaming, and sleeping states, but only a fortunate few, the yogis, attain the fourth state, called *turīya*. These rare ones reach the summit and have a profound view of all states experienced by human beings.

The aspirant who has attained such a lofty state is rare and knows the mystery of life here and hereafter. Nothing remains unknown to him. Such a great yogi does not belong to any caste, creed, sex, or ethnic group because he has already transcended all such superficial limitations. The knowledge that enlightens such an aspirant is called *Tripurā Rahasya*.

The text by that name is one of the most significant scriptures in the tradition of tantra yoga. Its beauty lies in the fact that it expounds the lofty knowledge of inner truth while systematically offering practical instructions on *śakti sādhanā*. In *śakti sādhanā*, the aspirant learns to apply all of his resources to the task of awakening the dormant fire within and leading it to higher awareness, finally reaching the highest *cakra*, the thousand-petaled lotus. In advanced stages of practice, the aspirant knows all about his future, even in the next life. This is the glory of *śakti sādhanā*.

The Tradition

Traditionally, spiritual knowledge was handed down from gurus to their disciples, and this tradition still exists. In ancient India it was customary for a student to know about the tradition and lineage of the knowledge he was receiving before he started treading the path of light. Thus, the *Tripurā Rahasya* opens with references to the tradition through which it has been transmitted. The seers Medhā and Sumedhā are said to be the spokesmen of this scripture—they made it available to the oral tradition and, from there, it was committed to writing. They received this knowledge from the sage Paraśurāma. Paraśurāma received it from Dattātreya, Dattātreya from Brahmā, Brahmā from Viṣṇu, and Viṣṇu from Śiva. In the *Mārkaṇḍeya Purāṇa* it is said that Medhā *ṛṣi* was also a teacher of the *Saptaśatī*, another prominent scripture of *śakti sādhanā*. Medhā *ṛṣi* was initiated by the great sage Paraśurāma, and so, in reciting the scripture, Medhā *ṛṣi* begins with the story of Paraśurāma.

Paraśurāma is one of the key links in the long chain of the tradition of the Himalayan sages. At one time, Paraśurāma stopped doing his austerities. He felt badly about his lapse and repented. In this frame of mind, he encountered a man who was pretending to be completely disorganized and mentally disturbed. The man ignored him, but Paraśurāma, determined to talk to him, made persistent efforts to get his attention. The man did not lose his temper, even though Paraśurāma teased him obstinately, but kept on smiling, mumbling something that Paraśurāma did not understand. This behavior convinced Paraśurāma that he had encountered a great sage who had conquered lust and anger, and so he surrendered himself at the man's feet. Seeing this, the man said, "I am Bṛhaspati's brother, Saṁvarta. I renounced my home in my childhood and began practicing contemplation. I protect myself from people by posing as a lunatic. I remain in contemplation all the time and have no time to teach you. Go to the sage Dattātreya, and he will initiate you in the worship of Tripurā."

Hearing this, Paraśurāma went to Gandhamādana Mountain, where the revered Dattātreya lived. This mountain is north of the Himalayas. In this calm and tranquil setting, he found someone seated in a meditative pose who greeted him with a smile, saying, "You are in the right place. The sage Dattātreya is seated in the inner chamber of this ashram. You may go in."

Paraśurāma entered and saw the sage. A courtesan was seated next to him, trying her best to charm him, and a goblet of wine was by his side. Paraśurāma was completely bewildered by this, but he had faith in Saṁvarta. Reminding himself that sages have their peculiar ways, he prostrated and sat in front of Dattātreya.

The sage welcomed him: "O Paraśurāma, you have taken the path of enlightenment. To attain perfect control over sense gratification is the way of victory. To have control over the palate and the sexual urge is a great achievement. As you see, I keep the objects of enjoyment with me—both wine and courtesan are by my side. Seeing this, all the sages have left me. They despise me now. For what have you come? Do you not hate me?"

Paraśurāma replied, "I have heard about you from the sage Saṁvarta, and have come to your feet with great *śraddhā* [faith]. Kindly instruct me."

Sage Dattātreya was happy to comply and imparted the knowledge of *Tripurā Rahasya* in the traditional manner. Having received this knowledge, Paraśurāma departed for Mahendra Mountain to do his *sādhanā.* This phase of his *sādhanā* lasted twelve years, and according to the tradition, it was during this time that he initiated Sumedhā *ṛṣi.* The text of the scripture translated in this volume begins at the end of this twelve-year period.

Initiation

Śakti sādhanā is not possible without initiation. Just as the Vedas cannot be studied without *upanayana saṁskāra* (initiation into the sacred thread), *śakti sādhanā* cannot be done without formal initiation by the master. In *śakti sādhanā,* the yogi awakens the dormant *śakti* power of his disciple through *dīkṣā* (initiation). There are various levels of initiation, and it is given according to the aspirant's state of mind and level of awareness.

It is important for seekers to thoroughly study the *Tripurā Rahasya* under the guidance of a competent master who has attained the knowledge of this scripture. To become qualified for the guidance of such a master, the student must have developed three qualities: first, he should be endowed with firm faith; second, he should be free from the attachment of "mine and thine"; and third, he should have a burning desire to attain pure knowledge.

The Text

The *Tripurā Rahasya* explains all the stages of enlightenment and inspires the student at every step. Other scriptures only talk about certain principles and tell the seeker what to do and what not to do, but they do not explain how to be. This scripture furnishes both the principles and the practices.

Another unique aspect of this scripture is that it is ascribed to a female deity. In the *Tripurā Rahasya,* through the worship of and devotion to the Mother Divine, the aspirant fathoms all levels systematically and finally attains the highest state of consciousness. Most other scriptures use the word "He" or other pronouns in the masculine or neuter gender when referring to God. But the *Tripurā Rahasya* uses the word "Mother" and other feminine-gender terms when referring to the highest deity. A child finds comfort in his mother's lap and is very close to her. It is easy for a child to converse with its mother and to learn from her. Similarly, in *sādhanā,* the seeker finds that his practice is easy and spontaneous when he uses the words "Mother," "*Śakti,*" "*Mahāmāyā,*" or "Tripurā Sundarī."

This highly practical scripture also reminds an aspirant that without *saṅkalpa śakti* (firm determination), neither philosophical knowledge nor spiritual practice has great value. It is through *saṅkalpa śakti* that one gathers the courage to tread the path. *Bhakti* (devotion) is also needed, for without it spiritual practice becomes dry and technical. In order to acquire the virtues of *saṅkalpa śakti* and *bhakti,* an aspirant must cultivate positive thinking—a virtue of a purified and sharpened intellect.

When the faculty of discrimination is sharpened, *saṅkalpa*

śakti strengthens. *Saṅkalpa śakti* is a prerequisite for entering the subtle realms within. Without it, one cannot tread the path of *bhakti*. *Bhakti* means compassion plus devotion. When the seeker equips himself with these two exquisite qualities, he is fully prepared to tread the path.

Firm faith develops in the company of the sages, by contemplating on the *ātman,* and by practicing the systematic method of meditation, described below:

First, learn to sit still, keeping the head, neck, and trunk in a straight line, yet remain relaxed.

Second, practice withdrawing the senses from the objects of the world by fixing the attention on the flow of the breath. Make the mind aware that the breath and the mind are like two sides of the same coin; they are inseparable, twin laws of life. It has been proven scientifically that when the mind is agitated, the inhalation and exhalation also become agitated, and jerks, shallowness, and several other inconsistencies appear in the flow of the breath.

The next step is to realize the nearness of the self within. This is accomplished by gearing the mind and its modifications one-pointedly to the individual self only. *Upāsanā* (literally, "to be near") means to be constantly aware of the self within. This is the prime goal of that *sādhanā* which leads the seeker to the highest state of attainment.

Upāsanā, or devotion, has two aspects—external and internal. In external worship, objects such as flowers and fruits are used and rituals, such as the fire ceremony, are performed. In internal worship, the mind and its modifications are made one-pointed and inward. Then, as the *Yoga Sutras* say, *tadā draṣhtuḥ sva-rūpe avasthānam*—the seer is established in his own nature.

The Schools of *Śakti Sādhanā*

There are three main schools of *śakti sādhanā*: *kaula, miśra,* and *samaya,* which correspond to the mental state and preparedness of the aspirant. All are concerned with awakening the kundalini energy from its dormant state at the base of the spine and leading it to the crown *cakra*.

Kaula is a highly systematic method of spiritual discipline which uses objects—such as *yantras* and mandalas—as a means of spiritual unfoldment, incorporating them into complex rituals designed to bring the senses under control. Adherents of this school concentrate on awakening the divine force latent in the *mūlādhāra cakra* (the root *cakra*).

Miśra means "combination." It is a midpoint between *kaula* and *samaya* and it is here that the student begins the transition from external to internal worship. In this school, the student masters the symbolic meaning of the *yantras* and mandalas and learns to internalize them with devotion. The master imparts the systematic method of leading the kundalini force to the *anahata cakra,* the heart center, which becomes the center of concentration.

Samaya is the highest of the three schools and is practiced only by accomplished yogis. The word *samaya* means "I am with you." When the aspirant attains this state, he feels as though he is walking in Brahman-consciousness all the time. His *ajapā japa* becomes spontaneous and effortless. Even in deep sleep, he remains aware of his mantra, because mantra becomes the predominant factor in all activities of life.

This school leads the aspirant directly to *mokṣa,* liberation. At this stage, the body is regarded as a living shrine in which the divine force dwells. All practices are internal. No internal method, such as contemplation or meditation, can be accomplished without establishing perfect harmony between the mind and the breath, and the aspirant is given breathing practices to establish this harmony.

When the aspirant is fully prepared and yet still encounters obstacles, the master bestows his grace. Through his kind touch or gaze, the master gives the aspirant his power. This rare occurrence is called *śaktipāta*. It is not possible to bestow *śaktipāta* on the masses, as a few modern teachers pretend to do.

In all three schools of *śakti sādhanā,* the awakening of kundalini *śakti* is the central theme, and initiation is given step by step. The highest initiation is called *mahāvedha.* In *mahāvedha,* the final knot of ignorance is cut asunder and the aspirant has access to the highest knowledge.

Tantra

The technique of attaining the goal of *śakti sādhanā* is called tantra. This is a method of helping one to realize the *ātman.* Etymologically, the word is derived from the verb *tan,* which means "expansion" or "introduction," and the suffix *tra,* which means "protection" or "guide." Thus, tantra is the path of *sādhanā* which leads an aspirant to the highest state of protection, which is the highest state of attainment. Tantric scriptures expound the multifarious meaning of all the *tattvas* (principles), from the Absolute to the manifest world, including the science of mantra.

The philosophy of Sāṅkhya is related to *śakti sādhanā* or *āgama* scriptures. It furnishes three types of evidence—direct experience, inference, and the sayings of the adepts—as does *śakti sādhanā.* Sāṅkhya also accepts the teachings of the Vedas. According to Sāṅkhya, one can attain freedom from sorrow and pain by knowing *tattva jñāna,* the knowledge of both the gross and subtle forms of the universe.

The profound knowledge of life here and hereafter is attained through *sādhanā.* An aspirant knows that there is nothing that actually goes to complete annihilation. No object is subject to destruction; that which we call death is a change of the form and name of that which is considered to be dead. When the body drops, the individual soul is still carried by the vehicle manufactured by desires (the unconscious mind). As long as it drives that vehicle, it is called the individual soul. The moment it drops that vehicle, it becomes one with the Absolute, in the same way that a river meets the ocean and becomes one with it.

In the *Tripurā Rahasya,* the dialogue between Śrī Dattātreya and Śrī Paraśurāma leads the aspirant to know what is duality and what is Absolute, One Without Second—what is *dvaita* and what is *advaita*. The state of *advaita* cannot be discussed, but can only be realized. Discussions are possible only in the state of duality.

About This Translation

Pandit Tigunait, being a scholar of Sanskrit, translated the *Tripurā Rahasya* in a manner that was very terse and scholarly. Therefore, it was not accessible to modern students, especially those in the West. After a careful reading of this translation, Deborah Willoughby and I recommended that he modify it so that it would be accessible to the general reading public, especially those on the path of *sādhanā*. Although this meant that he had to retranslate the entire scripture, I advised him to do so because a scholarly, abstruse translation would be of no use to the general reader.

The *Tripurā Rahasya* is one of the most wonderful and practical of all scriptures and is very helpful to those on the path of self-realization. I am certain that those aspirants who study this scripture in its present translation, with full faith and a tranquil mind, will have a new vision and will become aware of a completely new dimension of life.

1

The Quest of Paraśurāma and the Grace of *Gurudeva* Dattātreya

1. HOMAGE TO THE ABSOLUTE REALITY, the source and embodiment of bliss, the supreme consciousness, here termed as She, the Mother, who is both the magnificent image of the universe and the mirror in which this dazzling reflection appears.

2. The sage Hāritāyana asked, "O Nārada, have you listened carefully to the canto extolling the glory of the absolute reality known as Tripurā? Just listening to it is one of the most definite means of achieving liberation.

3. I will now tell you the wondrous *jñānakhaṇḍa* of the *Tripurā Rahasya*. After listening to it attentively a *sādhaka* is no longer subject to grief.

4-5. This philosophy was developed after studying the Vedas, Vaiṣṇaivism, Śaivism, Śāktism, and Pāśupata. There is no other philosophy that can be comprehended by the intellect as easily as this which Dattātreya taught to Paraśurāma.

6-7. The teaching imparted here is based on logic and reasoning. If, after receiving this knowledge, a person still does not comprehend it, he is indeed unfortunate.

8. And now I shall narrate the knowledge expressed in this canto of the *Tripurā Rahasya*.

9-10. The behavior of the enlightened ones is beyond the comprehension of ordinary people. That is the reason why a sage like you delights in these stories filled with wisdom. As the musk deer emanates its fragrance, similarly, such enlightened sages influence the life of many, particularly those who are on the path."

Paraśurāma heard the *māhātmyakhaṇḍa* from the mouth of Dattātreya.

11. Paraśurāma's heart was purified, overwhelmed by divinity, utterly calm and tranquil; his attention became one-pointed and inward for a while.

12. He then regained normal awareness. Tears flowed from his eyes and his whole body vibrated, for his heart was overflowing with spiritual bliss.

13. His heart was not able to contain that overwhelming bliss. With all humility, he prostrated at his guru's lotus feet.

14. When Paraśurāma gained awareness, he spontaneously uttered, "O *gurudeva,* through your grace I am blessed, I am blessed.

15. You, the ocean of compassion, Śiva himself, have blessed me. Your blessings are incomparable.

16. When the *gurudeva* is pleased there is no difference between mortality and immortality.

17. I consider that I have received the mystery and attained the essential knowledge of the Mother Divine, Tripurā, by your grace.

18. O lord, from you I have known the mysterious knowledge of Mother Divine and received her grace. I want to dedicate myself to the Mother of the universe. Please show me the way of devotion."

19-22. Dattātreya observed that Paraśurāma was fully prepared and endowed with firm faith and devotion, so he initiated him step by step into the worship of Tripurā.

One auspicious day, Paraśurāma received the initiation of Tripurā, that which leads to the highest. As a honeybee collects nectar from various flowers, Paraśurāma gathered from his master all the means and methods of *sādhanā.*

Overwhelmed with joy, he received permission from his master to return to the mountains to perfect the science of Tripurā.

23. He circumambulated his master with reverence, took his leave, and went to the mountain called Mahendra.

24. There he built a beautiful and comfortable shelter and engaged in *sādhanā* for twelve years.

25. While following his daily *sādhanā,* he devoted himself to worship, mantra *japa,* and meditation on the goddess Tripurā with a one-pointed mind.

26. Twelve years passed as if in a moment. Then one day, while sitting cheerfully, Paraśurāma began thinking.

27. "Long ago, while the sage Saṁvarta and I were walking together, Saṁvarta answered my question about the glory of Tripurā. At that time I did not understand the significance of his words.

28. I completely forgot what he said, so I could not confirm it by asking my *gurudeva.*

29-30. I requested my master, Dattātreya, to reveal to me the mystery of the universe (the true nature of the goddess Tripurā). He considered my question irrelevant and ignored it. So my question remains unanswered.

31. I do not know the secret of the universe. From where did this vast universe appear?

32. How can it exist? And where will it rest after its final dissolution? Everything seems to be unstable.

33. How can a relationship with any impermanent object last? All worldly activities seem confusing and mysterious.

34-35. The behavior of the ignorant is like the blind following the blind. My own life is an example of this. I do not remember what happened in my childhood at all.

36. I was a different person as an adolescent, still another person in my youth, and now my behavior is completely different.

37. What the result of all those changes is, I do not know; nor do I understand the cause of the relationship underlying changes; nor do I remember what happened, at what time, and by what means.

38. Has anyone ever received what he really wanted from his so-called right actions? Has anyone ever attained happiness from action? Did anyone ever become happy?

39. Whatever a person thinks he wants is not his desired object at all, because after obtaining it, he suddenly wants something different.

40-41. If one has attained the fruits, then why does he desire the fruits again? I see that everyone is doing his duty for the purpose of obtaining the fruits.

42. The fruits can neither give freedom from sorrow nor bestow happiness. As long as karma still remains to be performed, there cannot be freedom from sorrow, nor can there be happiness.

43. Just as it is in vain to treat someone dying of thirst by rubbing cold sandalwood paste on his feet, it is equally senseless to try to gain happiness by running after worldly pleasures. Therefore, one whose duty remains to be accomplished can never be happy.

44. If a man's chest is badly injured by arrows, he will not enjoy the embrace of even the celestial damsels. How can one whose worldly duty is not over expect to gain happiness?

45. How can the best of music and song bring cheer to one who is in agony from an incurable disease?

46. In reality, those who are free from the burden of their karmas are happy in the world. They are joyous sages; they are tranquil within and without.

47. If one is burdened by karmas, how is it possible for him to be happy? If one is going to be hanged to death and is honored by a beautiful lei of sandalwood, will he be comforted?

48. Oh, it is astonishing that a person who is caught in the

snare of worldly obligations actually believes that this trap is the prelude to happiness and conscientiously carries out those duties.

49. How can I honor people who consider themselves to be happy while burdened by innumerable obligations?

50. Both an emperor and a beggar constantly search for peace and happiness.

51. Their concepts of happiness are different. One is happy by acquiring a kingdom, the other by receiving a coin. Both consider themselves to be blessed.

52. Dropping this idea, shall I go to my revered *gurudeva* and request the solution to my problem? This is indeed an act of auspiciousness.

53. The words of my *gurudeva* will help me cross the ocean of delusion."

54. Paraśurāma set out immediately from Mt. Mahendra to see his *gurudeva.*

55. Soon he arrived at Mt. Gandhamādana, and there he saw his master seated in the lotus posture, like a self-illumined sun.

56. He prostrated in front of his master's wooden sandals. Then holding the sandals on his palm, he reverentially placed his head on them.

57. Accepting Paraśurāma's reverential greeting with appreciation, Dattātreya lifted him with compassion and blessings and embraced him.

58. "Son, I am seeing you after a long time. How are you? Are you healthy?"

59. Received thus, Paraśurāma sat down on the cushion and after saluting his *gurudeva* reverentially, began to speak,

60. "O *gurudeva,* ocean of compassion, how can one who has received your grace suffer from misery?

61. I am fully protected by the shield of your grace. Then how can this cruel misery come near me?

62-64. I feel your grace within and without. Separation from you is the only pain I have, and now after being in your presence, that has vanished. But something has lingered in my heart for a long time.

65. Because of that, my mind is always full of doubt. With your permission, may I ask you to resolve this?"

66. Hearing this, the compassionate Dattātreya joyfully said,

67. "Paraśurāma, ask whatever questions you have. Delighted with your devotion, I will answer them happily."

In this way the dialogue between the sages Dattātreya and Paraśurāma ends in perfect harmony. This is called jñānakhaṇḍa.

2

Sage Paraśurāma Makes Queries and His *Gurudeva* Replies

1-2. ON RECEIVING INSTRUCTIONS from his *gurudeva,* Paraśurāma bowed and inquired, "O lord, my spiritual master, knower of all, compassionate one, you know that many years ago I became enraged with the members of the royal family.

3. Twenty-one times I destroyed the ego and killed all the *kṣatriya* kings of the world. It was done for a specific reason.

4-5. I pleased my ancestors by doing this. My ancestors became happy. Receiving instructions from my ancestors, I became calm. During those days Rāma, the incarnation of Viṣṇu, was at Ayodhyā. In my pride, I created a serious conflict with him.

6-7. The Lord Rāma defeated me. He was kindhearted and a great devotee of the brahmins. Therefore he spared my life. After the defeat I became disgusted with the world, and repented.

8. On the way home, suddenly I met the great sage Saṁvarta. He was completely covered by ashes, exactly as embers are covered. It was difficult to recognize him.

9. His company gave me immense relief and a sense of abiding peace, just as a mist refreshes a man overheated by the midday sun.

10. I asked how he maintained this state of tranquility. He

imparted the essence of all scriptures and spiritual teachings.

11. But just as a beggar has no capacity to receive the immense treasure of the goddess Lakṣmī, similarly, I could not assimilate the knowledge he imparted to me. When I again requested him to instruct me, he sent me to you.

12. In the end, I have come to your lotus feet. In your presence I feel happiness, as an ignorant person feels joy in the company of the wise.

13. Though I did not grasp what the seer Saṁvarta told me, I listened as you described the glory of Tripurā. This enabled me to develop faith and devotion in her worship.

14. You are a symbol of the goddess Tripurā. That symbol is always in my heart. In this state of mind, what fruits will I not receive?

15. But even so, please explain what the sage Saṁvarta told me so many years ago, because without that knowledge I cannot be satisfied.

16. Without understanding his teachings, everything I do seems to be like the play of a child.

17. Long ago I worshiped the god Indra and other *devas,* and in those ceremonies gave them costly gifts and grains.

18. But I heard from Saṁvarta that the fruits of these pious actions are of little value. If they are insignificant, will I be sorrowful?

19. Not only is the absence of happiness painful, but pain mingled with joy is also painful.

20. The path of rituals does not help one face his great fear. An even greater fear is the fear of death, and there is no escape.

21. Even though I am engaged in the practice of Tripurā, I feel this fear because the way I worship Tripurā, the Mother Goddess, is not satisfying. It is like the play of my mind. Therefore I regard it as child's play.

22. The way you instructed me to worship the Goddess is

contradictory to other scriptures. The way rituals are performed differ from each other.

23. Apart from that, rituals differ according to the deity through which one worships, and there are various ways of worship. Therefore when a ritual is performed incorrectly, it does not give fruits exactly the way fruits are obtained from the fire ceremony.

24. If the entire ritual is false, then how can it lead to truth? Furthermore, these rituals are never-ending.

25. But I observed that the revered sage Saṁvarta was fully tranquil and completely free from the desire for self-gratification.

26. He seemed to be completely free and in a state of bliss. He followed the path of fearlessness. He looked like an elephant sitting quietly in a forest pool in the midst of a conflagration.

27. How did he attain that state which he talked about to me?

28. Please, *gurudeva,* tell me this secret. I am burdened by worldly obligations and responsibility. Please rescue me."

29. Saying thus, Paraśurāma placed his head at his master's feet to express his gratitude and respect.

The sage Dattātreya recognized his student's inspired state and realized that he was at last prepared to undertake the path of enlightenment.

30. The compassionate sage Dattātreya responded, "My son, your mind is fully purified.

31. Attaining such a high state is like a drowning man who encounters a boat.

32-33. By performing *sādhanā* and having devotion, great people attain a highly auspicious state. Mother Divine, though formless, assumes a form and can manifest herself for the sake of her devotee, and by enlightening him can give freedom from the bondage of death.

34. As long as one is not free from the evil of his karma, he is not happy. He remains disturbed, as if on the verge of death.

35. How can one whose every limb is burning with poison be happy?

36. The whole world is overwhelmed by the sense of duty and remains senseless and blind. Therefore, people of the world are not aware of what is good for them.

37. Without knowing the ultimate goal of life, human beings blindly perform their actions and thus keep walking in the darkness of ignorance. Actions performed blindly simply perpetuate the cycle of birth and death.

38-40. Once upon a time, some hungry travelers were searching for fruit on Mt. Vindhya. Believing they had found some cashews, they ate poison fruit instead, which made them extremely thirsty. Suffering from the effects of these poisonous fruits, those ignorant travelers then searched for something to quench their thirst, and mistaking some intoxicated fruits for grapefruit, ate them too.

41-42. Disoriented by the effects of these intoxicating fruits, they lost their way. Some fell into ditches and were injured.

43. Thorns pricked them. They blamed each other for their mishaps and started fighting.

44-45. Covered with wounds, they finally arrived at a city. It was midnight by the time they reached the town gate.

46-47. The gatekeepers would not allow them to enter. Oblivious to time and place, they fought with the guards and were again badly beaten.

48-49. Running here and there, some fell into a deep moat and were trapped and eaten by crocodiles. Several fell into pits or wells and died. Only a few escaped.

50. Similarly, people of the world run after tantalizing objects, constantly inviting misery, but in their delusion they persist in their race toward destruction.

51-52. Paraśurāma, you are very fortunate; that is why these earnest inquiries have arisen in your heart. *Vicāra* and tranquility are the first rung on the ladder of the highest attainment. To attain tranquility is essential. How can one gain the auspicious height without it?

53. Negative thoughts are like death. Only by understanding the auspicious goals will people stop running after trivial objects and finally become victorious.

54. The demons who roam in the night go to destruction because of their negativity, while the *devas,* because of their positive attitudes, become deserving of happiness.

55. Those having calm minds surrender themselves to lord Viṣṇu and remain victorious over their enemies. Positive thought causes joy, in the same way that a seed sprouts into a leafy tree.

56. With positive thoughts, a man goes ahead of others, and because of his positive power, Brahmā is considered to be higher. Because of his positive power, Viṣṇu is worshiped everywhere.

57-58. Through his positive brilliance, Lord Śiva is all in all. Though Rāma, prince among men, was deceived by Marīca and suffered heavily, later, by using the strength of his positivity, he created a bridge across the ocean and conquered Lanka, the city of demons.

59. This has been explained to you. Negative thought feeds the ego and that is why Brahmā had to lose one of his heads.

60. Similarly, Lord Maheśa in his spontaneity gave a boon to Bhasmāsura and, disturbed, ran from one place to another.

61. By not using his positive power, Viṣṇu killed the wife of the seer Bhṛgu. Bhṛgu cursed him and he had to suffer.

62. Similarly, many demons, *devas,* and human beings, under the influence of negativity, had to face problems.

63. O Paraśurāma, blessed are those who maintain tranquility of mind in all situations. Those revered ones should be adored.

64. For lack of positive thought, people perform their duties and remain caught in the snare of delusion; thus they become victims of innumerable miseries.

65. For ages, human beings have been caught in the web of negative thinking. As long as they are under the influence of that negative power, how can they think positively?

66-67. How can one find cool water in a burning desert? Without spiritual means, how can one think harmoniously when his mind is negative and scattered? There is only one spiritual *sādhanā* to overcome this problem. For building that positive attitude, there is only one way, and that is higher than any other means.

68. Discrimination dawns through the grace of Tripurā. Without the grace of the one who dwells in the inner chamber of the heart on the lotus therein, how can anyone attain the blissful state?

69. The light of consciousness will dispel the darkness of ignorance, and the means to attain it is devotion with firm faith.

70. The great Mother Divine is the subject of worship when, by her grace, she is seen as the self-illumined one in the depth of the heart.

71-72. The supreme goddess is identical with one's own self, the knower of all, the most resplendent pure consciousness, and the embodiment of auspiciousness.

After being initiated by a realized teacher, one should follow the path sincerely and systematically. On the path of spirituality, devotion and faith are essential.

73. O Paraśurāma, I have already taught you the rare scripture on the grace of Tripurā, which is the root of this knowledge.

74. By hearing her extolled you attained her grace, the root of all goodness. Therefore, you will have no fears at all in the world.

75-76. As long as positive thinking does not arise, a person remains fearful in daily life. Even after the cause of fear is removed, some degree of fear still persists, just as a person recovering from a serious hallucinatory disease still suffers from weakness.

77-78. However, the purpose of life is accomplished when one develops the capacity to discriminate and is always aware of his spiritual goal. If, after achieving human birth, one fails to cultivate positive thinking, the tree of human life does not bear fruit, just as a barren woman does not give birth to a child. Success is attained by positivity.

79-80. Those who are devoid of positive thought are narrow in their thinking, like frogs in a well; a frog born in a well lives without knowing the difference between day and night. Similarly, a human being without a positive attitude takes birth uselessly.

81. He is not aware of what is beneficial or harmful for him. He goes through the round of births and deaths again and again without trying to discover what is truly beneficial.

82. Under the influence of ignorance, he mistakes pain for pleasure and pleasure for pain. Thus, he is continually burned by the flames of worldly desires.

83-84. People suffer but never seek an end to suffering. A female donkey kicks the male again and again, yet he still follows her. Similarly, people lead their lives in the world. Thus, O Paraśurāma, people do not renounce the world. You are endowed with pure intellect and you have crossed the ocean of delusion."

Here ends Chapter 2, with the dialogue between the great adept Śrī Dattātreya and the sage Paraśurāma.

3

The Meeting of Hemacūḍa and Hemalekhā

1-2. HAVING BEEN TAUGHT by Śrī Dattātreya, Paraśurāma wonders, and humbly puts the question, "O lord! revered *gurudeva!* What you have said is true. People invite their own destruction by their negative attitudes.

3. They can attain what is auspicious through positivity, which will lead them to listen to the glory of the Goddess. I have heard it, but I have a serious doubt.

4. How does one gain the opportunity to hear about Tripurā? If this happens naturally in the course of events, then why has everyone not heard of her glory?

5-6. Why was I not interested in learning about her before this moment? There are many people who are more miserable than I am, who should be more motivated to turn to Tripurā. Why do they not have the opportunity to know this subject? Please help me to understand this."

7. "Listen, Paraśurāma. *Satsaṅga,* the company of the wise, is the way to attain the absolute good. It dispels the darkness of ignorance.

8-9. The company of the wise yields the most desirable fruit.

You, yourself, attained this higher state that leads to the greatest good through the company of the leading sage, Saṁvarta. Sages find joy in the company of other great sages.

10-11. Without the company of a sage, who could ever attain the highest bliss? Even in worldly life, a person sees the effects of the company he keeps. Now listen, Paraśurāma, I will tell you a story.

12. Once upon a time, there was a king of Daśārṇa named Muktacūḍa. He had two sons, Hemacūḍa and Maṇicūḍa.

13-14. They were both handsome, intelligent, and skilled in many sciences. One day, equipped with bows and escorted by their army, they went hunting in the forests of Mt. Sahya.

15-16. Soon their sharp arrows had brought down many deer, tigers, boars, buffalo, and wolves. As they were hunting, a tornado raged through the area, showering everything with debris and rocks.

17. The sky was full of dust, and day appeared as dark as night. It became so dark that they could not see the hills, trees, or even each other.

18-19. The whole mountain was engulfed in darkness. The troops, wounded by the hailstorm, scattered. They found shelter under trees and boulders or in caves, while the two princes fled on their horses.

20-21. Eventually Hemacūḍa, the elder prince, arrived at a beautiful hermitage surrounded by banana and date trees. There he saw a lovely girl as radiant as a flame, glowing like molten gold.

22-23. Seeing that beautiful maiden, as enchanting as the goddess of good fortune, the prince smilingly inquired, 'O lotus-eyed girl, who are you, dwelling in this forest fearlessly? Why are you living in this wild and lonely place? Whose daughter are you? With whom do you live? And why are you all alone at this moment?'

24-25. The beautiful girl replied, 'Welcome, prince. Please take your seat. It is the duty of an ascetic to welcome guests. You look tired and worn.

26. Tie the horse to the tree of dates, rest, and be comfortable and hear my story.'

The prince complied with her request.

27-28. She served him fruit and juices and after he had relaxed awhile, the girl spoke to him with honeyed words. 'O prince, there is a sage named Vyāghrapāda, who is a staunch devotee of Lord Śiva.

29. Through the power of his austerities, he has conquered spheres of reality won only by those with the highest virtues. He is a knower of the absolute reality and was endowed with the knowledge of Brahman. Many great sages used to attend him.

30-31. My name is Hemalekhā, and I am his adopted daughter. Once upon a time, a charming and beautiful celestial girl named Vidyāghrī went to bathe in the Venā River. By chance, during that time, the king of Vaṅga was present there.

32-33. He saw that beautiful girl bathing in the river. Because of her wet clothes, her breasts were visible. Charmed by her beauty, the king gently approached her, and she agreed to his proposal.

34-35. After making love with her, the king returned to his capital, without being aware that the girl had become pregnant. Fearing criticism, that beautiful girl abandoned the infant.

36. The sage Vyāghrapāda happened to be passing by on the way to his evening meditation. He took me to his hermitage, and raised me with love and care.

37. A father is one who fulfills his duty by taking care of his children. I am his daughter and serve him.

38-39. Because of his spiritual greatness, there is no reason for me to have any fear. Neither gods nor demons with their evil thoughts can enter this ashram, for if they were to approach, they would be destroyed. That is my story, O prince. Please stay and rest for a while.

40. My father, Vyāghrapāda, is about to come. Wait and pay homage to him and he will fulfill your desire. Then early tomorrow morning you may proceed.'

41. After listening to her, the prince, overwhelmed by her beauty, wanted to speak to her, but he became nervous.

42. The astute young woman understood that the prince had fallen in love with her and said, 'O prince, have courage and wait.

43-44. My father will be coming very soon. Wait until he arrives, and then request that he give you my hand.' As she spoke these words, the great sage entered with the flowers and fruit he had collected for worship. On his arrival, the prince got up with reverence.

45-46. Introducing himself, he bowed his head reverently and sat down again only with the sage's permission. The sage noticed that the prince was bewildered because of the lust in his mind, for he used his yogic power and assessed the situation. He gave the prince Hemalekhā's hand.

47-49. Overjoyed, the prince took her to his capital. With pleasure, his father married them according to the Vedic rites. The prince began enjoying his married life, sometimes in the forest, sometimes on the banks of the river, and sometimes in other places. But to his dismay the prince noticed that his bride was not interested in sensual gratification. She always seemed indifferent.

50. Finally one day he gently said, 'Darling, I love you, but you do not seem to respond to my love.

51. Your smile is very charming, but why do you not find delight in lovemaking? Does it not please your heart? Why are you sad?

52. You seem to be indifferent. How can I enjoy you, when you are so detached?

53. I am fully devoted to you, but it seems that your mind is always elsewhere. When I speak to you, I feel you have not heard.

54. I have been sitting here for a long time embracing you, but you have not noticed, and you ask me, "Lord, when did you come?" as though you were unaware of my presence.

55. You have the best of enjoyable objects in front of you. Even so, you do not think of them. Why do you not express yourself?

56. When I am not with you, you start meditating. I notice these things whenever I see you.

57. If you have no appreciation for worldly pleasures, then tell me how I can enjoy myself, for I feel like a man embracing a wooden statue.

58. I will fulfill your wishes. As the lily opens its petals in moonlight, similarly my heart is opened to you.

59. You are dearer than my life. Why are you indifferent? Swear upon God, so that my doubt is dispelled.'

Thus ends Chapter 3, with the dialogue between Hemalekhā and Hemacūḍa.

4

The Awareness of Hemacūḍa

1-2. BEING EMBRACED BY THE PRINCE and hearing him, with an innocent smile Hemalekhā said, 'Listen to me, my love. It is not true that I do not love you.

3. But I am constantly preoccupied, trying to decide what is the best and most joyful thing in the world and what is not. I cannot understand what is right and what is wrong.

4. For many days I have been brooding on this, but being a woman, I cannot find a satisfactory answer. Please let me know the solution.'

5. The prince laughed at her remark and told her,

6-7. 'Even animals, birds, and insects sense what is pleasant and what is not. They are naturally inclined toward what is pleasant and repelled by what is unpleasant. What is there to brood about? The things that give you joy are pleasant; the things that do not are unpleasant.

8. My love, you are very innocent. Why are you so perplexed about this subject?'

9. Hemalekhā replied, 'You are very brilliant, so please help me understand. Women by nature are weak in their decisions, but you can decide; therefore please counsel me.

10. Once my ignorance is dispelled, I can stop worrying and enjoy life with you.

11. Dearest, you are such a deep thinker. You have explained to me that things from which one attains pleasure and pain are pleasant and unpleasant, respectively.

12. I am confused, however, because the same object that is a source of pleasure one moment causes pain the next. So how can I decide what is pleasant or unpleasant?

13-15. For example, in winter a fire is pleasant, but on a hot summer day it is intolerable. A fireplace is always welcome in a cold climate, but in tropical countries it is not needed.

16. The same principle applies to one's wealth, spouse, children, kingdom, and every other pleasing object. For example, your father is graced with a wife, children, and wealth.

17-18. Then why is he worried all the time, while those who do not have wealth like you do not worry? No object is able to give you joy forever and ever. No one's desire is ever fulfilled, and no one is happy.

19. Lord, this is not joy at all, because it brings suffering. There are two kinds of pain: external and internal.

20. Disturbance of the humors causes pain in the body. Conflict causes pain in the mind, for the mind is filled with desire.

21. Pain of the mind is intense. Because of it, the whole world is in bondage. Desire for enjoyment is the cause of pain.

22. Those who are slaves of desire always suffer. Even the *devas* in heaven work constantly to fulfill their desires.

23. O prince, even after enjoying the desired object, craving does not diminish. Actually, real pleasure is impossible to attain.

24-25. Nature regulates the life of the animal kingdom, but the hearts of human beings remain laden with the desires for sense gratifications. If they can be fulfilled, then all will be happy in the world. But that's not true.

26. If a person suffering from fever can be relieved by cool water, then a person with desires can also be happy.

27-28. It is said that the embrace of a woman is enjoyed by men, but if it is a rough embrace, it is painful. After making love, people feel exhausted.

29-30. O lord, tell me the secret of how to transform this pain into pleasure. Do dogs not experience the same kind of gratification that a man does with his lover? If you argue that a man experiences more pleasure than an animal because he sees the beauty in women, that is untrue.

31. The perception of beauty is in the beholder's eye, and is no more than a dream. Listen, here is a story: Long ago there was an extremely handsome prince.

32-33. His wife was exquisitely beautiful, and could easily capture any man's heart. The prince was very devoted to her, but she was secretly involved with one of the servants.

34. The servant would give the prince a large quantity of liquor to make him drunk. After he was senseless, the servant would send an ugly maid to sleep with him, while he himself made love to that beautiful princess.

35-38. For a long time the inebriated prince continued sleeping with the maid, believing he was enjoying the company of his beloved wife. He used to consider himself the most fortunate man in the world. Then one day the servant poured the liquor and left, but for some reason the prince did not drink as much as usual.

39-40. Excited by desire, he hurried to the royal bedchamber. The bedroom was beautifully decorated. Like Indra, the king of gods, rushing to meet his wife, Saci, the prince hastened to his room and joined the maid asleep in his bed.

41-43. The prince made passionate love with the woman he found there. Then as he calmed down, to his astonishment he discovered that she was not his wife but an ugly maidservant. He was infuriated and he wanted to know where his wife was. The maid realized that the prince was sober, and kept silent, trembling with fear.

44-47. The agitated prince caught hold of her hair in his left hand, and picked up his sword with his right. Angrily he shouted, "Tell me the truth or you won't live another moment!" In order to protect herself, the terrified maid revealed the truth. Then she brought him to his wife, who had been making love to the servant.

48-51. The prince saw his wife lying on a mat spread on the ground, in the embrace of the servant. The servant was tall, ugly, and dirty, and was exhausted from lovemaking. The princess's arms were wrapped around his body like a creeper. The servant was embracing her. They looked like a thorny vine intertwined with flowers.

52. The prince saw his wife in deep sleep and for a moment was overcome by love and desire. He thought: I should be ashamed of myself for getting drunk.

53. Shame on those who indulge in sexual activity and lose their senses. Men say women change their love and fly away, but in reality, men are polygamists.

54-55. What can I say to myself? I was stupid. I loved her dearer than my heart. I'm ashamed of myself. As the beautiful birds do not sit on the same tree every day, so the beautiful women do not belong to one man. But who am I? I am like the calf of a buffalo, completely engrossed in attachment, and so far I have loved to live this way.

56. As a courtesan does not love one person, so is the nature of women. One who trusts them is like a wild donkey.

57-59. It is amazing. Until now I did not understand the nature of women. I loved my wife dearly, but still she abandoned me. She was having an affair with another man but hid it. Like an actress who expresses her undying love to an actor in a play, she pretended to love me.

60. I was under the influence of liquor and did not even know with which woman I slept. I always thought my wife was my faithful companion.

61-64. Under the influence of liquor, I slept with that ugly woman. Who on earth could be more stupid than I, who was duped for such a long time? What beauty did my wife see in that treacherous servant, whose features I find so ugly, that she would actually agree to make love to him? She preferred him, even though my good looks attract the eyes of all, and I was fully devoted to her.

65-67. During the course of this inner monologue the prince became disgusted with the world and, breaking off all attachments, left to live out his days in the forest.'

Hemalekhā continued, 'O prince, thus you can see that so-called beauty is merely skin deep; therefore, it is in the eye of the beholder. Just as you experience pleasure by seeing my beauty, people find pleasure even in unattractive women. Sweetheart, I am going to explain. Please listen carefully.

68-69. The mind assumes an image of the beloved according to the concept therein, and a time comes when the image and object become one.

70. When the mind is restless, the senses are also distorted. But when the mind is fully one-pointed, it is neither excited nor distorted, but is in a state of equilibrium.

71. The image within it is imagination. The infatuation repeats the mental image, but yogis or children remain unaffected because their minds are free of the imagery.

72-73. One finds enjoyment according to one's own concept of beauty. All husbands love their wives, no matter how ugly they are considered to be, and they have children.

74. Superficial human beings, whose minds always think of sexual activity, find pleasure anywhere, without discrimination.

75-76. A lustful and distracted man projects beauty onto an unattractive body. If a person can see beauty in the human body, which is a gross object, then anything can be considered beautiful.

77-78. O prince, beauty is an idea, which comes out of the womb of desire. Beauty lies in the beholder's mind and spontaneously flows to the object of love, but the tender minds of children do not recognize it, for they are free from lust.

79-80. The color and figures of people differ in different races, countries, and times. The concept of beauty differs according to race and culture. The faces and limbs which seem distorted to one person are considered attractive to another.

81-82. People have many different complexions; the definition of beauty differs accordingly. O prince, everyone, though having external differences, seems to enjoy the same pleasures.

83-84. Even the best of men find pleasure in a woman's company because she is considered to be delightful. Equally, a man's beauty attracts a woman and is enjoyable to her. O prince, learn to understand this.

85-86. When one analyzes the components of the body, it has all sorts of decaying elements and it is hopelessly disgusting. A seeker should know this.

87-88. Those who find delight in pleasures of the body are like animals. O prince, this body is full of unpleasant elements. The one who thinks of every part of the body gets disgusted.

89-90. The same is true of food, even though it has different flavors. Even the most delicious food becomes waste material.

91. After reflecting realistically on the nature of the human body, please tell me, what is pleasurable and what is not.'

92. Hemacūḍa was surprised at his wife's views. The truth of her remarks changed his attitude toward the world.

93. Pondering her words, he lost interest in objects of enjoyment and developed non-attachment. In the course of time, he asked many questions and came to understand the highest truth.

94. Gradually he realized that one's own *ātman,* blissful Tripurā, resides in everyone's heart. With this realization he gained freedom and was able to see the entire universe in his own self.

95-96. Through his knowledge, both his father and younger brother also attained liberation. The queen, Hemacūḍa's mother, attained knowledge from her daughter-in-law, and then gradually the knowledge spread to the ministers and finally to the common citizens.

97. No one in that city remained ignorant. They all attained freedom from worldly craving. That city seemed a veritable city of Brahmā, Brahmapurī.

98. The capital became the best in the world. Even the parrots and *sārikā* birds, while sitting in their cages, spoke in the following manner:

99. 'Pure consciousness devoid of objects is one's own real self, the *ātman*. Contemplate on that. External objects are not different from consciousness.

100. Consciousness alone is the object of its own awareness. I am that consciousness. It alone is the entire universe. All this is experienced through consciousness by the illumination of the self.

101. O people of the world, cast off your confusion by focusing your minds only on consciousness. Worship and meditate on Her. Consciousness is the illuminator as well as the source and support of all.'

102. Hearing such sermons coming from parrots, the great sages renamed the city.

103. They announced, 'Because here even birds discuss the supreme knowledge, henceforth this town will be called Vidyānagara, the city of wisdom.'

104. The city is still known by that name even today. Thus, Paraśurāma, the company of the wise is the most effective way of attaining the highest good.

105. Thanks to the presence of Hemalekhā, all the citizens gained wisdom. So you see, Paraśurāma, the company of the wise is the main source of liberation."

Thus ends Chapter 4, with the dialogue between Hemalekhā and Hemacūḍa.

5

The Helplessness of Hemacūḍa and the Wondrous Sermon Given by Hemalekhā

1. AFTER HEARING THIS PRAISE of *satsaṅga,* the company of the wise, Paraśurāma humbly inquired,

2. "Lord, you mentioned that the company of the wise is the root cause of success in spiritual life. This is true. I have had direct confirmation of this in my own life through the company of the sage Saṁvarta, which resulted in my spiritual quest.

3-4. A person is known according to the company he keeps. People attained greatness merely by associating with Hemalekhā. Indeed she was a great woman. I want to hear in detail how she led the prince to the highest truth."

5-6. "Then listen to that divine story," Dattātreya began. "After listening to his wife, the prince lost interest in external objects and became non-attached to the world.

7. Habits make deep grooves in the mind, and it becomes difficult for one to enjoy a life of spiritual freedom.

8. Because of his male ego, the prince kept his emotions hidden from his beloved. He passed the time in a mental dilemma.

9. Even when his habits led him to his old ways, he was still aware of his wife's words and was ashamed of himself.

10-11. The old habits forced him to go back to his previous

saṁskāras, and again he repented. His mind went into the old grooves formed by his habit patterns and he brooded on the sayings of his wife.

12. The time came when he lost interest in the best of food, clothes, jewels, and beautiful women. No charm of the world could interest him.

13. He lost his mental equilibrium, as if his entire fortune had been stolen, but because the subtle yearning for pleasure lingered in his mind, he could not renounce all objects entirely.

14-15. Yet, after seeing the imperfection of worldly things, he did not care to enjoy them. He became gloomy. Hemalekhā noticed and asked him privately, 'Why do you not look as happy as you did before?

16. You look sad all the time. Why are you in such a pathetic condition? Do you have a physical illness?

17. According to the wise, the body is subject to disease. It is made by air, bile, and phlegm; an imbalance in any of these three constituents can lead to disorders.

18. Disease produced by imbalance affects the whole body. Restoring the natural balance is difficult.

19. Irregularities pertaining to food, speech, sense activities, time, place, and physical activity disturb equilibrium.

20. Though the cause of these disturbances ordinarily is difficult to know, there are many ways of treating such diseases.

21. If such imbalances of the humors did not exist, no one would have described the various ways of curing numerous diseases. Therefore, tell me what is the cause of your agony.'

22-23. The prince replied, 'Darling, I will tell you the cause of my anguish. After I listened to your discourse, the things that previously appeared pleasant no longer seemed so. I do not find anything in the world that gives me joy.

24. Though the king has furnished me with the objects of luxury, they do not cheer me any more than pleasurable objects can console a man about to be hanged.

25. Yet, I crave worldly objects because I am still a slave of the subtle tendencies of my mind. Darling, what can I do to be happy?'

26. Seeing her husband's anguish, Hemalekhā realized that because of her previous discussion with him, the prince was beginning to develop dispassion.

27. He had the potential for spiritual growth; otherwise the dispassion would not have unfolded in him, for a philosophical discourse cannot make the least impression on those who do not desire liberation.

28. Only after prolonged devotion, when the goddess Tripurā bestows her grace, can a person attain the highest state.

29-30. The wise Hemalekhā revealed the wisdom of Tripurā to her beloved husband. With measured words, she imparted the secret wisdom to the prince. Then that great learned lady, without exposing her learning, started telling her husband this story:

31. 'O prince, this has happened to me. My mother gave me a maidservant, whose nature was fairly good. Later on, she associated herself with a bad woman.

32. This bad woman was both creative and crafty, and I associated with her without my mother's knowledge.

33-34. The maidservant was very dear to me. Overpowered by the influence of her crafty companion, I started misbehaving.

35. Because I thought of my maidservant constantly, I became like her. That wily witch tempted my maidservant with beautiful but worthless objects.

36-38. In secret, she turned my maidservant over to her son Moha (attachment), who was always drunk and had bloodshot eyes. Moha became her lover. He would often forcibly enjoy her, even in front of me. She was possessed by him, but she never abandoned me. Therefore, I became involved with him, too. They eventually had a son, Asthira (unsteady nature), who was stupid like his father.

39. This son was born in an adult body. He was very unstable

and inherited all the evil qualities from his ancestors.

40-41. He spontaneously developed a talent for drawing all kinds of pictures. Although he was already clever, his father and grandmother educated him further and helped him to develop his skills. His activities were very creative.

42. My maidservant, though essentially pure, was influenced by the company of that wicked woman.

43-45. She became attached to her lover and son and began living with them. I could not break our friendship because I was too attached to her. I could not develop self-reliance; thus I became dependent on her.

46. Her lover tried to play with my emotions, but I did not heed his crafty suggestions. Pure by nature, nobody could persuade me.

47. Rumors spread far and wide about me, and the people of the world started thinking that I was involved with that wretched man.

48. My maidservant left that unsteady son with me and remained in her lover's embrace forever.

49. I started to bring up that unsteady youth. Then, inspired by his grandmother, he established a relationship with an adult woman.

50-51. His fiancée, Capalā (ever-moving, ever-changing), could metamorphose at any moment, taking the most amazing and surprising forms at will. Through her great craftiness, she controlled her lover.

52. That unsteady one was able to travel innumerable miles in a moment. He would never tire, yet he was always restless.

53-54. Whenever and wherever he wanted to visit his fiancée, he appeared there instantly. She entertained him by assuming any form he fancied.

55. Living with that unsteady youth, she had five sons, all devoted to their parents, and all having distinct characteristics. My friend gave them into my care.

56-57. For my friend's sake, I helped them become even stronger and more powerful. Those five sons built huge and beautiful homes. Then, aided by their mother, they dominated their own father.

58-62. They called their father whenever they wanted. Once the father visited his eldest son's residence, where he heard the sweetest of melodies, enchanting instruments, and other pleasant sounds. Sometimes he listened to the chanting of the Vedas and the tantric texts, and sometimes to the tinkling of jewelry or the sweet song of the cuckoo. He was delighted living under his son's control, and being constantly exposed to pleasing and harmonious sounds. But, later, that same son turned against his father.

63-64. The father was distressed to hear the roar of menacing animals such as tigers, the thundering blasts of storm clouds, and the lamentations of many people.

65-67. Another time, his second son took him to his home, where he was offered a comfortable seat, bed, and clothing. There he found things with the qualities of hardness and softness, and heat or cold. Pleasing objects were joys for him, but unpleasant sensations made him sad.

68-70. He visited the residence of his third son, where he saw objects of many colors. They had multiple shapes. Some were nice and some were dreadful.

71-76. Among them, some were disgusting, some bright, some exciting, some full of darkness. While he was observing these various objects, the fourth son invited him to his house. At this son's home, he found different kinds of fruits and delicacies. There he ate many delicious things. Some of these were as sweet as nectar, some sour, salty, bitter, astringent, or pungent. While he was enjoying these various tastes, his last son brought him to his house and presented him with many kinds of flowers.

77-79. There he experienced the fragrance of many plants. Some were fragrant and some stank; some had mild aromas, while others were too strong. Some smells were pleasant to the senses, others were refreshing, and a few were overpowering. In this way he experienced numerous objects. When he experienced something pleasing he wanted to retain it, but exposure to unpleasant things frustrated him. Thus, he continued visiting his sons.

80. The sons were very much devoted to their father. Without him, they would not go near enjoyable objects.

81. But sometimes when the unsteady father was enjoying himself in his son's homes, he would steal some objects and take them home.

82-85. There he would share them with his wife, Capalā. After some time, one of his wife's sisters, Mahāśanā (unsatiable one), seduced him, and he married her also. Now that unsteady man became attached to his second wife and was forced to supply many kinds of objects in order to make her happy. She would instantly consume whatever he would bring and demand even more. Enticed by his wife, he was constantly busy.

86. His five sons brought objects, but she would devour them and be hungry again in a moment.

87. She made her husband and his sons supply her with many objects of enjoyment. Soon she had two sons of her own.

88. One of them was Jivalamukha (fiery mouth) and the other was Nindyvṛtta (immoral character). She loved them very much.

89-94. Often the unsteady father suffered and fainted while embracing his fiery-mouthed son. He was frequently slandered because of the conduct of his corrupt son. He became miserable. Out of attachment, my maidservant sympathized with her unsteady son and keenly felt his pain. Gradually she became attached to her two grandchildren also. She almost died because of them. I was always with her. Therefore, darling, I also was lost and was plunged in untold misery.

95. I remained miserable for many years, suffering because of the misery of my maidservant. By then her unsteady son was fully enslaved by his second wife.

96-100. One day he departed for a city that had ten gates. He lived there with his mother, his second wife, and their sons. He wanted to be calm, but day and night he was in misery. Attached to his two younger sons, he had to face terrible suffering and condemnation. He got tired of constantly visiting his other five sons. He never experienced a moment of tranquility.

Suffering from her son's deeds, my maidservant nearly collapsed. Yet, in this condition, she lived with her husband, daughter-in-law, and grandchildren in that city.

101. Her foolish father-in-law, her husband's grandmother, his in-laws, and her husband's other wife nourished her.

102. While she lived in that city, she was completely dominated by her husband. Because of my love for my friend, I also lived there, doing everything for her.

103. Although I almost died because of my friend's suffering, I protected her whole family. Sweetheart, without me they could not have survived. I protected them all.

104-5. However, under the influence of ignorance, I lost my equilibrium, became unsteady and fickle, and desiring enjoyments, identified myself with the objects of enjoyment. When I kept the company of Moha, I became stupid.

106. Due to the company of my maidservant, I had to play many roles. Had I left her, she would have died.

107. Because I was in bad company, the stupid men thought that I was a corrupt woman. But good men thought otherwise.

108. My mother was holy. She was free from negativity, both mentally and physically. She was more pervasive than space and more subtle than the atom.

109. She had profound knowledge. Even so, due to the absence of egoism, she pretended that she knew nothing. While doing everything, she acted like one who did nothing. She was the source of all, and at the same time self-existent. She was fully detached, though she was the very basis of all.

110. Although she was formless, she could assume all forms.

In the midst of everything, she remained untouched. She was present here, there, and everywhere, but was unnoticeable.

111. She was full of bliss yet was not noticeable, and she had no parents. Of course she has innumerable children.

112. Like waves of the ocean, I have innumerable sisters. O prince, we behaved alike.

113. I am endowed with the highest power of mantra. That is why I live and sympathize with my maidservant and sisters, yet am pure like my mother.

114. In that city, whenever the unsteady son of my friend got tired, he would rest beside his mother.

115. Whenever he slept, all his children also slept. No one remained awake.

116. During that sleep period, only Pracāra, a friend of the unsteady one, would travel back and forth through the two eastern gates to protect the city.

117-19. My friend would sleep beside her unsteady son. At that time my friend's mother-in-law and the immoral seductress would cover and protect them. Whenever they slept I would slip away to my mother. Embracing her, I would be filled with joy. The moment they awoke, I instantly returned and was caught up with them again.

120-21. Asthira, the unsteady son, had a close friend named Pracāra, who looked after the whole city. He was only one, but had many forms and was popular in the city. He protected everyone and always helped them contact the objects of joy.

122-23. Without him, they would fall apart like the beads on a necklace after the thread snaps. Working with me, Pracāra kept that city alive. He inspired and maintained the whole city.

124-27. When the city became ancient and began to crumble, he led them all to another city. In this way, under the protection of Pracāra, the unsteady one became the inhabitant of different kinds of cities. Although the unsteady son was born of a holy mother, was supported by the powerful Pracāra, and nourished by me, he was miserable all the time. He never abandoned his two wives and seven children, though they tormented him.

128-29. He continued suffering and never found peace. His sons kept dragging him in different directions. Under the influence of his two wives, he had no occasion to rest.

130-31. Affected by his fiery-mouthed son, he would faint from fever, and no remedy could cure him. At other times, in the company of his corrupt son, he was the subject of vicious slander and nearly died of shame.

132-34. Because of his disreputable nature, he restlessly moved from one city to another. Each city had a different character. Sometimes he was forced to live in the open surrounded by wild creatures, sometimes he lived in cold, dirty, or dark places.

135. In this way, living in bad company, my maidservant suffered due to her attachment to her son.

136. Sweetheart, even though I was pure, because of the association with her family, I was influenced and thus became sad.

137. Who in the world can be happy while living in bad company? This is just like a person who is trying to quench his thirst with water from a mirage.

138-39. In this way the time passed, and my friend, in deep sorrow, spoke to me privately. Through me, she found a good husband. Thus, she was able to purify herself and control the negative thoughts and emotions.

140-41. In my company she became aware of the Mother Divine and, overwhelmed by her presence, attained freedom. After that, she was in bliss all the time; bliss became an inseparable part of her life.

142. O prince, only by attaining inner wisdom can eternal happiness and the Divine Mother's grace be obtained. Now I have imparted the way of attaining bliss. This is my direct experience.'

Thus ends Chapter 5 with the teachings of the bondage and release of Hemacūḍa.

6

The Doubts of Hemacūḍa and the Teaching of Hemalekhā on Firm Faith

1. HEARING HIS BELOVED WIFE SPEAK, Prince Hemacūḍa was astonished and still unsure. He did not know that she was an enlightened being. Smiling, he asked her,

2. 'Sweetheart, everything you said seems to be like building a mansion on sand. Your speech and facts do not match.

3. You are the daughter of a celestial nymph and were brought up by a *ṛṣi*. You have just recently reached your adulthood.

4. But the events you are describing would take generations to occur. You talk like a woman possessed by spirits.

5. There is no consistency in your story. What can I possibly make of it? Tell me where this maidservant of yours is, and the son who captivated her?

6. Tell me where that city is. Or forget all this and just tell me, where is that maidservant?

7. I did not meet any maid. My mother is in the palace—go ask her. My father has only one wife.

8. Tell me immediately where such a maid is to be found and where her son is. You are talking in parables, like that of a barren woman who claims to have a son.

9. Your story reminds me of the comedian in a drama who

claimed, "A barren woman's son is riding a chariot reflected in a mirror.

10-11. He is wearing silver ornaments made from the shiny inner surface of a shell. He killed a king who had not yet been born with weapons made from human horns while fighting in a forest in the sky. He also conquered the mythical city of the Gandharvas and is enjoying dream-women from the dream city."

12. Your story makes as much sense as this one.' Hearing him, that brilliant woman spoke again,

13. 'Lord, how can the things I have told you be false? My parables are not false.

14. Speaking untruth destroys the austerities. How can one see beauty in leprosy and how can one born in a family of truthful people tell lies?

15. The man who diverts the mind of a seeker by lying can never attain happiness in this world or the next.

16. O prince, hear me attentively. One with defective eyesight can not regain his eyesight by merely pronouncing the words of the remedy.

17. An ignorant person considers helpful advice to be worthless. How can I, your beloved wife, lead you, who sincerely wants to find the truth, to the unreal?

18. Even if my statements are utterly contradictory, you can understand them through the help of your subtle and discriminating intellect. People are accustomed to making judgments in their daily activities.

19. By examining a few details, they understand the whole situation. To help you think clearly about this, let me remind you of one of your own experiences.

20. After having listened to me the other day, why are the objects that previously provided pleasure unpleasant to you now?

21. They still provide pleasure to others. Now you can determine the validity of my story.

22. O prince, I am telling you the truth. Please listen to it humbly. Not trusting a trustworthy person makes one his own worst enemy.

23. Firm faith is a mother. She protects those who take refuge in her, as a compassionate mother protects her own child in all difficulties.

24. That fool who does not have firm faith in the teachings of the self-realized ones loses wealth, happiness, and reputation. A person without firm faith remains ignorant.

25. It is firm conviction that sustains the whole and is the life of all. Tell me, how could a child survive without having full faith in his mother?

26. How can a young man be happy if he does not trust his wife? How can an old man rest peacefully if he has no confidence in the younger generation?

27. How can a farmer till his field if he does not believe in the harvest? Without faith and trust, no one will bother to either collect or renounce the things of the world.

28. Without trust and truth, the world will crumble. If you say the world functions without faith, that is not true.

29. Predicting future events on the basis of past experience requires faith in the causal relationship between past and future.

30. Without faith, no one can even breathe. So cultivate firm faith and use it to attain sublime happiness.

31-32. If you think that one should not rely on stupid people, then listen. This thought is based on faith in their unreliability.'

After hearing her brilliant sermon, the prince asked again,

33. 'Hemalekhā, according to you, faith is necessary for spiritual growth. You say that I must develop faith in wise people so that I can attain the state of auspiciousness.

34-35. One who wants to attain the highest good should not trust the wicked or he will be victimized. Those who seem good on the surface may be crooked inside and may deceive us, like the fish who becomes the victim of an alluring worm wrapped around a fisherman's hook. Therefore, one should discriminate between the wise and honest, the wicked and deceitful.

36. There are many examples of those who created problems for themselves by trusting someone unwise, and those who got out of difficulties by having faith in the wise.

37. But the question is, how can you be certain your judgment about whether people are wise or wicked is correct? Your judgment itself requires scrutiny.'

38. Being challenged in this manner, Hemalekhā answered her husband, 'O prince, listen to me.

39. First, decide whether a man is good or bad.

40. Even if you have arrived at that conclusion by having firm faith in great men, this conclusion is still subject to confirmation by the signs and symptoms we see in them. Thus, firm faith will be subverted by reliance on signs and symptoms, as explained in the scriptures.

41. If you say that the characteristics of a good man are described in the scriptures, then I ask, how can you believe in the scriptures if you have no faith?

42. If, on the other hand, you do not trust the scriptures, but you accept the reliability of people's statements, then the advice of a human being will be your basis for believing or not believing in something. However, the statements of all humans are not unanimous; therefore, people should have firm conviction, but the validity of that conviction must be confirmed by the scriptures.

43-46. I am explaining to you the means of attaining the highest goal of life. Please listen attentively. Neither those who involve themselves in mere logic nor those who do not reason at all can attain the goal here and hereafter. Long ago, in the direction of Sahya Mountain, there was a sage named Kauśika living at the bank of the Godavari River. He was very learned. There were hundreds of students under his guidance.

47. One day in the absence of the master, those students began arguing about the nature of the universe according to their intellectual knowledge.

48. During that time, a highly educated brahmin named Śuṅga arrived. He used his mental skills and defeated all of them in debate.

49-52. Lacking faith in the scriptures, that brahmin had lost his intuitive wisdom. However, he was an adept debater with great power of discussion. The students all agreed that whatever can be elaborated through evidence must be true. Then Śuṅga said, "Brahmins, listen. You claim that whatever can be proved through evidence must be considered true. But in this way truth can never be proven, because if the evidence is inconclusive, the conclusion derived from it will be faulty too. Therefore, first one must evaluate the evidence.

53. The evidence has to be validated through some other proof. In order to determine the faultlessness of that new proof, one must depend on still other evidence. Thus, a logician falls into the fallacy of infinite regression, and nothing at all can be directly shown to be true.

54. Therefore, the thinker, the object, and the source or means of knowledge can never be proven. The conclusion we come to is *śūnya,* the void.

55. Yet, the void cannot be proven without reliable evidence. Trying to prove the void ends in void."

56. Impressed by these arguments of Śuṅga, the students with shallow knowledge followed him, accepting *śūnyavāda* (the philosophy of the void).

57. Because of their confidence in Śuṅga, they got lost in the jungle of this philosophy and ruined their lives.

58-59. But there were a few discriminating students who presented the views of Śuṅga to their learned master and received a proper answer, which dispelled their doubts. Therefore, only one who abandons mere logic and who reasons with the assistance of the genuine scriptures attains the higher state.'

60-61. Hearing his wise beloved, Hemacūḍa was even more surprised and finally admitted: 'Darling, you are so learned. I did not know it before. You are blessed, and I am blessed because I have your *satsaṅga.* All that is attainable can be attained through firm conviction. How do you acquire that?

62. Where should one place his faith and where not? There are numerous scriptures that seem to contradict each other.

63. There are even differences among preceptors and commentators about a single scripture. Also, one's own intellectual convictions vary from time to time. Therefore, what should one accept or discard?

64. Every teacher considers his opinion to be valid and often refutes others' opinions, claiming them to be unconvincing.

65. Because of this, one cannot reach a definite conclusion even through the scriptures. For example, the teacher who proclaimed *śūnya,* the void, to be the supreme reality considered the theories of the others to be faulty.

66. His statements concur with the scriptures belonging to his own philosophical school. So why should we not rely on those statements? I believe you have already considered this question. Therefore, sweetheart, please help me understand clearly.'

Thus ends Chapter 6, with the description of the importance of firm conviction on the path of enlightenment.

7

Contemplation and Different Methods of Worship

1. AT THE REQUEST OF HER HUSBAND, Hemalekhā, who knew the mystery of the universe, continued explaining,

2. 'O beloved, compose yourself with reverential attention. I will answer your questions. The mind is like a monkey, jumping incessantly.

3. Because of such a mind, people ordinarily get caught in damaging activities. A scattered mind is the cause of pain.

4. The mind in deep sleep is without contents and is a cause of pleasant experiences. Please listen to me with a one-pointed mind.

5. That which is heard by a disgusted mind is as good as not heard at all, like a tree in a painting that cannot bear fruit.

6. When a person abandons mere logic and begins believing in his own convictions, he gains the desired fruits.

7. Therefore, one should practice *sādhanā* with the help of pure reason. After attaining the faith born of pure reason, a person achieves everything here and now.

8. O dear, renounce this useless logic. All the activities of this universe are based on *śraddhā* [firm faith], and *śraddhā* alone is helpful.

9. With determination, at the right time the farmer tills the land. Similarly, discarding the useless uncertainty of the mind and by having faith, people make decisions regarding the value of silver, gold, gems, and medicine.

10-11. One should be aware of one's ultimate goal, as the scriptures explain, and then make sincere efforts on the path of *sādhanā*. Logic is without foundation. Unlike Śuṅga, one should not abandon his duty.

12. Effort made with firm faith never fails. How can one miss the goal if he is working with firm faith and making sincere efforts?

13-14. With faith and effort, farmers grow crops, businessmen earn money, kings vanquish enemies, intellectuals study, laborers work, the gods drink ambrosia, and meditators realize the Absolute. Nothing can be achieved without sincere effort.

15. Think carefully and tell me: Has one without faith who does not think reasonably ever attained the desired goal?

16. A man who has a skeptical nature and is without conviction can never receive the desired fruits of his actions. He is his own enemy.

17. One must have immense faith supported by right reasoning and sincere effort if he is to select the means for attaining the highest good. Make use of the means you have.

18. There are various methods for attaining the goal. Whatever you feel to be appropriate, consider that to be the way for yourself.

19. According to the scriptures and one's own experience, one should start practicing *sādhanā*. I will tell you these secrets. Please listen to me attentively.

20-21. That which removes sorrows should be considered the highest good. If one observes subtly, he will find sorrow everywhere in the world. That which is mingled with sorrow cannot be the highest good.

22-23. Wealth, son, wife, kingdom, treasure, strength, fame, worldly knowledge, intellect, and physical beauty are all impermanent. All these objects are deadly, as if located in the mouth of a poisonous snake.

24. Because of attachment to wealth and other objects of the world, there is delusion—delusion arises out of attachment. Attachment leads to misery.

25. The highest good is not born out of the delusion arising from wealth and other worldly objects. Maheśvara is the cause of the universe, but because of attachment, people are not aware of that.

26. Even a magician deludes people through his skill. But his power is limited; he cannot fool everyone.

27. If ordinary people cannot see through the illusions conjured by a magician of limited power, then who can cross the mire of delusion created by Maheśvara, the supreme lord?

28. One who knows how to be free from illusion gets freedom from it. He can lead a perfectly healthy life and thus obtain all the joys.

29. But that knowledge through which joy is obtained is not possible without grace.

30. Without the grace of Maheśvara, how can the mire of delusion be crossed? Therefore, his grace is most essential.

31. After being blessed by him and attaining *mahāvidyā,* supreme knowledge, through his grace, one can cross the mire of delusion.

32. Advanced techniques of *prāṇāyāma* and other yogic practices are described in the scriptures as a means for attaining supreme knowledge, but without the grace of Maheśvara they cannot lead to the final goal.

33. Therefore, one should gain the profound knowledge of the Absolute. This knowledge enables yogic *sādhanā* to remove delusion.

34. Though no one has seen its emergence, the universe seems to be the work of someone. It is made of parts, and some

intelligence must have brought it into existence.

35. The origin of this universe is deep and profound. Therefore it is subject to investigation with the help of a purified mind and the sayings of the holy scriptures. With the help of these, one knows that the cause of the universe is not comparable to anything else.

36. Although some scriptures and philosophers say that this universe came into existence without cause, these arguments are invalidated by authoritative scriptures.

37. Sensory evidence does not lead anywhere. It will certainly never lead to liberation, and great men do not heed such evidence. Those scriptures that support such a theory need to be denounced.

38-39. Texts that profess mere logic should be discarded, because logic alone cannot lead to liberation. Some philosophers think the universe is without beginning and end. This cannot be true, because material objects are insentient, yet all actions are initiated by a conscious principle. Without consciousness, there can be no activity.

40. According to most scriptures, this conscious principle is the primal cause of the manifestation of the world.

41. Thus, both the scriptures and discrimination reveal that this universe is an effect of the activity of the conscious principle (Maheśvara). He, the doer, is separate from all worldly objects.

42-43. The nature of the universe is indescribable, for it is vast, a heaven of unimaginable diversities. Therefore the conscious principle, or primeval doer, is indescribable and has unlimited power and capacities. He is the source of all power and therefore can lead all seekers. He is the way.

44-47. I want to elaborate this point by giving an example,' Hemalekhā said. 'When employers are pleased with the honest service of their employees, they reward them accordingly. The Lord of the Universe is full of compassion, and all the desires of his devotees are fulfilled. A true seeker is desireless. Rich people are generally greedy, ungrateful, and lack compassion. Whatever is obtained from them is trivial and short-lived. But the merciful Lord, who is all-compassionate, is blissful. His grace is everlasting. The fruits received from such *sādhanā* do not decay.

48. If God is not like this, how could he remain unblemished? How could this universe be so well regulated?

49. The countries of kings whose administrations are not well managed fall apart, but the universe runs smoothly and seems well organized by the grace of the compassionate Lord.

50. There are two methods used by seekers for attaining the absolute reality: having desires, and being desireless. Those who surrender themselves without any hesitation are guided by providence.

51. Among many approaches to realizing God, the first is to remove the obstacles, the second is to gain the means, and the third is complete dedication and self-surrender. Self-surrender is the surest of all methods.

52. People of the world worship God to fulfill their desires. As a result, their mundane desires are fulfilled. However, the worship should be *sattvic.*

53. Sometimes they commit mistakes in their way of worship and become indifferent. Therefore such aspirants, laden with desires, receive limited fruits or the fruits remain uncertain.

54. But one who performs his worship selflessly gains mastery over all worldly objects.

55. The ignorant do not know the higher worship of desirelessness, but the Lord, being omnipresent, is the governor of everyone's heart.

56-57. He knows everything and gives the fruit immediately. Those whose *sādhanā* is full of desires receive the fruits according to the nature of their *sādhanā.*

58. The Lord of Life helps those who have successfully surrendered themselves to attain the highest goal.

59. The supreme Lord, Maheśvara, is kind and merciful and

always graces his devotees by fulfilling their desires.

60-61. The law of predestiny loses its power for the *sādhaka.* It is known that in the case of the great devotee Mārkaṇḍeya, the Lord blessed him with a rare boon. Let me explain the reason.

62. Karmic laws are inevitable, but a fortunate few remain unaffected by these laws because their karmas are already exhausted.

63. Life on this platform cannot be sustained without *prāṇa.* One can escape from the karma of his past lives by mastering the highly evolved practice of *prāṇāyāma.*

64. Those who are not spiritually oriented and do not practice are tossed inevitably by *prārabdha,* the past karmas that have started producing their fruits. This is the law of karma.

65. *Niyati* (the power of law) is a power of the Lord and its real nature is *saṅkalpa,* firm determination. The Lord is truth and firm determination; therefore the law cannot be dissolved.

66. This law is not applicable to the fortunate few or to exceptional devotees. This aspect of the law is like a bridge for devotees.

67-68. Therefore, dismiss polemics. Take refuge in Maheśvara. He will help you attain the highest good. In the ladder of attainment, bliss is the final rung and nothing else is worthwhile.'

69. O Paraśurāma, after listening to his wife, Hemacūḍa was delighted and continued his queries.

70-72. 'Darling, please describe the nature of this Maheśvara who is the ultimate refuge. The one who is the doer of all, absolutely self-existent, and the controller of the entire universe is known by various names. Devotees call him Viṣṇu, Śiva, Gaṇeśa, Sūrya, Nṛsiṁha, Buddha, Sugata, Arhata, Vāsudeva, Prāṇa, Soma, Agni, Karma, Pradhāna, Aṇu, and many other names.

73. The cause of the universe is described in various ways. Can you tell me where and how God-oriented *buddhi* is used?

74. I am sure that you know everything, because the great

sage Vyāghrapāda, your godfather, was the knower of all, and he has taught you everything.

75. That is why, being a woman, you have profound knowledge. Darling, you are as sweet as nectar and your teachings are helpful. Tell me the secrets, for I am a devotee.'

76. After being asked by her husband, Hemalekhā happily said, 'Lord, listen, I will explain about God.

77. The one from whom the world springs, who is responsible for the manifestation of the world and where it rests in the end, is God. The same is called Śiva, Brahmā, Sūrya, and Candra.

78. In all names and all forms, God alone is seen. He is beyond forms and the names of Śiva, Viṣṇu, and Brahmā.

79. Listen attentively. Now I reveal a great secret. *Śaivites* consider the five-faced and three-eyed Śiva to be the creator of the universe.

80. Pay attention—I will tell you. If the primal cause of the universe has five faces and three eyes, then that being, which has a form, is subject to change, death, and decay.

81-82. Mind functions in dreams without the help of the physical body to express its dormant desires. This indicates that a body is an instrument of the individual soul.

83. Human beings need instruments to express themselves, because of their limitations, whereas the creator of the universe, being perfect in itself, does not need any aid. This means that God is not any particular person.

84. Only God is sovereign and, without the aid of any other, has manifested the world.

85. Therefore it is concluded that God is never embodied in any form. Otherwise, he would depend on some sort of instrument in order to create the world.

86. The universe was never created, but was manifested. All these forms of the world have been manifested by him, yet he is beyond all names and forms.

87-88. God, being omnipotent, omnipresent, and omniscient, is the sovereign power, without a second. God cannot be perceived. He projects the universe.

89-90. The ignorant remain confused about formless absolute reality. In their ecstasy, they visualize the supreme in different forms. According to the nature of their devotion, God assumes various forms and fulfills their desires, though he is formless, absolute, and pure consciousness.

91. Consciousness is transcendental and is beyond all three states of mind—waking, dreaming, and sleeping—and is named Tripurā. Though this universe is inseparable from her, it appears to be separate and the same as Viṣṇu and Śiva. Therefore you should not consider them different. They are one and the same.

92. The entire universe is a reflection of pure consciousness. Consciousness is non-dual. Therefore, there is nothing superior or inferior.

93. It is in respect to lower states or forms of consciousness that people consider some forms of God to be more significant than others. They are but projections of the human mind. Therefore a wise man should worship or meditate only on the absolute state of consciousness beyond names and forms.

94-95. However, those who are not capable of comprehending the Absolute should selflessly and with full dedication worship God in any name or form that is pleasing to them. Even if one is born a million times, he will not find another way.

Thus ends Chapter 7, in which the nature of the Absolute is described both as formless and with form.

8

The Dialogue Between Sage Hemalekhā and Hemacūḍa Continues

1-3. AFTER LEARNING THE NATURE of the great goddess Tripurā, Hemacūḍa's mind became calm. Then he studied with learned masters from whom he understood the *saguṇa* form of the goddess, the form that has attributes. Blessed with the grace of Maheśvara, the great Lord, he began to practice meditation on Tripurā with full determination and dedication.

4. After several months of worship, grace dawned in him and his outward-oriented mind one-pointedly turned inward. Therefore, his mind became indifferent to pleasures.

5. This is not possible without the grace of God. When the seeker's mind is totally engrossed in the search for truth, then it becomes a means of liberation.

6. O Paraśurāma, countless may be the methods a seeker uses, but he will fail if the correct method for attaining truth is not applied.

7. Some time later he went to meet his wife. His mind was completely absorbed in the search for truth. Whenever Hemacūḍa saw his wife, his mind was inspired to attain truth.

8-9. When his wife saw him coming, she welcomed him and offered him a seat respectfully. Reverently, she washed his feet, prostrated in front of him, and spoke gently.

10. 'O lord, I have not seen you for a long time. Are you healthy? The body is prone to sickness.

11-12. How are you? You have not thought about me for a long time. You used to say you could not spend even one day without seeing me. How did you spend your time without me?

13-14. I know you would not go anywhere else without asking me, even in a dream. You would always say that a single moment without my company was like thousands of years. Please tell me, what has happened? How did you spend your nights without me?' With these remarks she embraced him.

15. In spite of her embracc, Hcmacūḍa did not feel any excitement. He told her, 'Sweetheart, you should not be attached to me like this.

16. I know you now. You have no cause to worry because you know the reality beyond cause and effect. You are the embodiment of patience. How can you be deluded?

17. Please explain the story of your life to me.

18. Who is your mother? Who were your maidservant and her husband? Who were her sons? And tell me, when did I come in contact with them?

19. I do not think I understand your story correctly, yet I cannot believe that it was a lie. Surely you were conveying something symbolically.

20. Please explain it to me clearly so I can understand it properly. I am very happy with you, but please remove the doubt from my heart.'

21. Hearing these words, Hemalekhā's face glowed. She felt that through the grace of the supreme being, the prince's mind had become purified.

22. Through the grace of the divine force he had patiently withdrawn his mind from worldly objects. His virtuous deeds were beginning to bear fruit.

23. Recognizing that the time for his self-realization was very

near, Hemalekhā decided to impart more spiritual wisdom. She said, 'Through the grace of the Lord, your good fortune has risen.

24. Without good karma, no one experiences indifference to material objects. This is the first symptom of the grace of the Lord.

25. The second symptom is becoming aware of the pettiness of the charms of the world through discrimination. Now I will explain the journey of the self, which I described to you before.

26-27. Pure consciousness is my mother. The intellect is my maidservant. Ignorance charms and distracts the intellect and is the great enemy of the faculty of discrimination. The power of ignorance is immense and can delude anyone.

28-29. Great attachment is the child of ignorance, which had an unsteady son called mind. His wife is imagination. He has five sons, the five senses: hearing, taste, sight, touch, and smell. Sense gratification becomes their *saṁskāra*. They dwell in the sense organs. Being embroiled with sensory objects becomes the habit of the mind.

30-31. The mind carries those objects back to its own abode to enjoy them in dreams. Expectation, the unstable glutton, is the sister of imagination. She produces anger and greed. Their dwelling place is the body, the city of life.

32. *Prāṇa* and mind are twin laws of life and function in tandem. Without knowing the highest purpose of life, this world becomes the source of pain and confusion for the human being.

33. The highest attainment, in which the mind with all its faculties attains a state of tranquility, is called *samādhi.* My admission into the inner chamber of my being is emancipation.

34. Thus, I have explained the story of my life, and your story is the same. May you be absorbed in *samādhi* and attain the highest good.'

Thus ends Chapter 8, in which Hemalekhā explains her parable to Hemacūḍa.

9

After the Sermon Given by Hemalekhā, Hemacūḍa Attains Enlightenment

1-2. HEMACŪḌA WAS AMAZED at this exposition and said, 'Princess, you are truly great. Your wisdom is immense. How can I praise the profundity of your teachings?

3. I have never heard such a story before. Now I can see its inner significance as clearly as if I were gazing at a small fruit on the palm of my hand.

4. Now I remember and experience that state within me. How amazing is life. But tell me, who is my mother, supreme consciousness? And how was I born from her?

5. Tell me who we are and what are we.'

O Paraśurāma, thus asked by Hemacūḍa, Hemalekhā replied,

6. 'Lord, I will reveal that deep secret: listen respectfully with a one-pointed and purified mind.

7. The self (*ātman*) cannot be preached or described. How can I explain? The moment you know your self, you will know your mother.

8. No one can teach you about the nature of the self, for the intellect through which a person thinks is also dependent on *ātman*. You can recognize the self only through that self.

9. The entire universe, from the grossest to the subtlest, is

known through the *ātman*. That *ātman* can be experienced only through knowledge but is never the object of knowledge itself.

10. It is beyond description, time, space, and causation.

11. Even the best of teachers cannot show you the light of your eyes. The self is realized by the glory of the self alone.

12. A master's role is only to reveal the path leading to the supreme reality. All I can do is show you the way to absolute truth. Be attentive.

13. Any object that you consider yours is different from your real self.

14-15. Go into solitude and discriminate what is you and what is not. The self lies beyond cognition. For example, I am your wife. I am related to you, but I am not you.

16. Renounce everything that you consider "yours." The self can never be renounced. By knowing the self, you will be liberated.'

17-18. Having received these instructions from his wife, Hemacūḍa mounted his horse and left the city. He reached his garden, as beautiful as the garden of Indra, in which there was a crystal temple. He entered the temple.

19-20. He left all his servants outside and ordered the guards to allow no one to enter while he was contemplating, not even the ministers, teachers, or his father, the king.

21. He climbed up to the ninth story of the temple. From there he saw the scene all around him.

22. He sat down on a cushion made of cotton, made his mind one-pointed, and began contemplating. During that time, he was all alone.

23-24. 'Why are people deluded? No one here knows about the self. People perform actions with the hope of enjoying themselves. Some of them are reciting the Vedas and some are studying the scriptures.

25. Some of them are busy accumulating money; the rulers

are engrossed in administration; others are embroiled in arts or indulging in sensual pleasure.

26. Although no one knows what the self is, people perform actions for their own benefit. Why is there such delusion?

27. Alas, without realizing the self, all activities are theatrical and in vain. So now I am going to contemplate on the self alone.

28. My palace, wealth, kingdom, wife, and cattle cannot be my self. They are mine, but none of these are me. Because of ignorance, I feel they are mine.

29. My body is my instrument. I am the son of a king, with healthy limbs and a fair complexion.

30. Everyone identifies himself with the body.' So far, the prince was identifying himself with his body. Body-consciousness should be transcended by understanding the fact that this body is mine and my real self is different from the body.

31-33. Eventually, he stopped identifying himself with the body, which is the basis of attachment. He thought, 'How can this body be the self? It is composed of blood, bone, and other components. It is ever-changing, like wood or a mountain, which decay.

Dreams are part of life, like waking and sleeping. If I am not aware of my body in the dream and sleep states, I cannot be my body. The same is the case with my *prāṇa,* the vital energy.

34. I cannot be my mind or intellect, either. My mind and my intellect are my instruments. Undoubtedly, every component of myself, from my body to my intellect, is different from me, the self.

35-36. No one experiences his non-existence. There is no doubt that I exist. But I do not know through what means I experience my own existence. Why do I not realize it directly?

37. All material objects are experienced through the senses, tangible objects through the skin and mental objects through the mind.

38-39. *Buddhi,* the intellect, can be distinguished through its decisive function. But how do I experience myself? I do not know.'

40-41. He was suddenly plunged into great astonishment. Having a glimpse of the self, he was exhilarated and started meditating intensely.

42. When the restlessness and conflicts of the mind were controlled, he saw light emanating from everywhere.

43. After the light vanished, he wondered what it was. 'Oh, why am I experiencing so many diversities?'

44. Curious, he controlled his mind once more, directing it inward. This time his mind slipped into deep sleep.

45. He shifted from deep sleep to the dream state, where he had many unusual experiences. On waking, he started thinking:

46. 'Was all of this a dream? Whatever light or darkness I experienced might have been the fragments of a dream.

47-48. Dreams are imagery in the mind. How can I go beyond them? Let me now make an effort to control my mind and its modifications.' He again made an effort and found himself in deep bliss.

49-50. After a while, his mind began functioning in the waking state. He wondered, 'What is all this about?' He could not discriminate between dream and hallucination. This experience was beyond his imagination.

51. 'This unique experience of bliss cannot be compared with the experience I had before. I felt as though I was asleep and not aware of the external world. I found this blissful experience peculiar.

52. I do not see any explanation for this. How did it happen? I was trying to realize the nature of the self, which still remains a mystery to me.

53. I see the *ātman* in so many different ways. What is all this, actually? Is it light, darkness, bliss, or something else?

54. Are these appearances of the self in different forms? I am

not able to reach any conclusion. Let me ask my learned wife. She understands these things.'

55-56. He then called for Hemalekhā to come to him. In an hour's time Hemalekhā arrived and climbed up the stairs, like the queen of night traveling in the blue sky.

57. There she saw her beloved husband, the prince, whose mind was tranquil, steady, and free from all modifications, and whose senses were completely withdrawn.

58-62. She sat down next to him. The prince opened his eyes to find his dear wife beside him. The moment he looked at her, she embraced him lovingly and spoke in a sweet voice. 'Lord, why did you call me? Are you healthy? Tell me the reason you summoned me here.'

The prince replied, 'Darling, after listening to your teachings I retreated here. To realize the self directly, I started contemplating.

63-64. I thought that my mind was focused inward, but actually it was not; I was aware of many things other than the self. I can differentiate between the self and non-self.

65. Then I saw darkness, light, and many other scenes, and occasionally I felt great joy. What was all this?

66. Was it the nature of the self or something else? Please explain it clearly so that I can experience it directly.'

67. At his request, Hemalekhā, the knower of truth, spoke gently about the world and beyond. 'My dear, listen to me.

68. Whatever effort you have made to control the external modifications of your mind is very good. All the adepts consider this to be one of the important ways of attaining the goal.

69. Without that, no one would have knowledge of the self. Self-realization does not need any evidence, because self-existent reality is present all the time.

70. If it is already present, why does it need to be attained? *Ātman* is not attainable through any state of mind. Direct knowledge of the self is the purpose of all *sādhanā*.

71. There is no moment when the self does not exist. That which is self-existent is not subject to attainment. Let me give you a few examples.

72. Suppose something is hidden in the dark. When the darkness is removed by the light of a lamp, then the objects are finally revealed. That is the case with *ātman.*

73-75. Suppose a person hides a cache of gold, and then forgets where he put it. He stops thinking about everything else and concentrates on finding the gold. In this way he finally remembers. This is how one "remembers" the presence of *ātman.* Avoiding thinking about other objects is not the reason that the man finds the gold. In the same manner, controlling the modifications of the mind is not the cause of the attainment of the self. You are not aware of the nature of the self; that is why you do not experience it directly.

76. A person who has never seen a lamp may visit a palace at night. He sees the light, as well as the courtiers, but does not recognize the source of the light.

77-78. Consider this: After controlling the modifications of your mind, you saw darkness. But before that darkness appeared, there was a brief instant of complete silence and an absence of all objective awareness, including the awareness of darkness. In that state in which you are entirely alone, you are only with your self. Always think of that state of experience—it is the source of supreme bliss. People with outward-oriented minds remain unaware of this state.

79. Learned and skillful seekers continue their search, yet do not attain that highly evolved state.

80. These seekers worry and become sad, for they do not know that state. Theoretical knowledge of the scriptures can never make anyone adept.

81. The philosophy of the self is not a mere theory, which is subject to discussion. Self-realization is beyond all argumentation.

82. Realization of the self is never attained by running here and there. Stillness is important.

83. No matter how far one goes, one cannot attain self-realization. That is attained through steadiness. Pure knowledge is not realized through mere contemplation. It is realized after renouncing all desires, but never by performing any action.

84. Just as one cannot capture the shadow of his own head by running after it, self-realization is not possible through any physical or mental effort. A child can see thousands of reflections on the surface of a clear mirror, but does not notice the mirror itself. Similarly, in the vast mirror of *ātman*, people see the entire universe reflected, but do not become aware of *ātman* itself.

85. Although a person is familiar with the concept of space, he will attend to the objects present in space, never noticing space itself.

86-88. My lord, think about this world of subjective and objective duality at an even more subtle level. The subjective aspect (knowledge) is self-evident, and without it, nothing can exist. Although knowledge of the self is the ultimate source of all valid knowledge, it is not the object of any kind of cognition.

89. One who denies knowledge has no ground to stand on. It is not possible to have a discussion with such a person.

90-91. Like a reflection in a mirror, everything shines in *ātman*. The knowledge of *ātman* is beyond the limitations of time or space. Self-luminous consciousness is the knower, and that alone is real. Just as space appears compartmentalized by physical objects, knowledge only appears to be limited by time and space.

92-93. O prince, the pure and still mind can realize the unity in diversity. By realizing the self, one becomes the self. Now I will tell you the means of attaining it.

94-95. By using your faculty of discrimination, observe the moment between dreaming and wakefulness, as well as the period between two thoughts. With the help of a calm and still mind, the state between sleep and waking can be understood.

96. In the real self there is no form, taste, smell, touch, or sound. There are no senses, either. There is no pain or pleasure; there is no loss or gain. That is the summum bonum of life.

97. Although it is the source of all, it is beyond all. It is the Lord of all, the creator, preserver, and annihilator.

98. Let a seeker stop the outgoing flow of mind by turning it inward and remain aware of the self, which is the self of all.

99. Learn not to identify yourself with your thought patterns. Then you will be witnessing the world and its objects as different from yourself. The time is short. Hurry up.'

100. Hemacūḍa followed the instructions imparted by his wife literally. For a long time, he remained constantly aware of the self. When he came out of *samādhi* he forgot the objects of enjoyment.

Thus ends Chapter 9, on attaining peace.

10

With the Teaching of Hemalekhā, the Whole City Becomes Wise

1. HEMALEKHĀ NOW REALIZED that her husband was established in supreme consciousness and left him undisturbed.

2-3. After a little while, he opened his eyes and saw his wife. But as soon as he tried to close his eyes and reenter that peaceful state, his wife caught hold of his hand and spoke to him sweetly.

4-5. 'O prince, tell me, what is your plan? What have you attained after closing your eyes and what have you lost by opening them? I would love to hear about your inner experience.'

6. Due to inertia, Hemacūḍa's mind was sluggish. He did not want to talk, and spoke with the lassitude of a drunken man.

7. 'Sweetheart, for the first time in my life I am at peace. I find no satisfaction in external activities.

8. These external activities are as tasteless as the pulp of sugar cane after the juice has been squeezed out. I do not need them. I was blind before and did not experience this transcendental peace.

9-12. Like the man who did not realize there was a treasure hidden in his house and who wandered begging, without knowing this ever-present bliss, I considered sensual pleasure to be satisfying and paramount. I see now that worldly pleasures are fleeting and laden with misery. I kept running after worldly pleasure without discriminating between pain and pleasure and did not find any peace at all. Alas, due to lack of discrimination, people find only pain and misery in the name of attaining happiness. I do not want to endure my self-created miseries anymore.

13. I pay homage to you with this respectful gesture of my hands. Be generous with me and leave me alone. I want only to rest in blissful *ātman.*

14. Alas, it seems as though you are unfortunate, because even after realizing this state, you are still caught, experiencing the pains of the world and not enjoying the bliss.'

15. That wise lady answered with a smile, 'My lord, you do not seem to have attained that pure state.

16. The state of knowledge in which a realized soul never again becomes deluded is far beyond your comprehension, exactly as the earth is far from the sky.

17. What you think you understand correctly is like no understanding at all. That self-illumined state of being cannot be seen either by opening or closing the eyes.

18. It cannot be attained by action or inaction, by renouncing home or living at home.

19-21. If it is attained by closing your eyes, doing something, or going somewhere, then how can it be supreme? That is poor knowledge, the awareness of which disappears when you open your eyes. How heavy is your delusion! What can I say about your amazing belief that knowledge of the absolute reality, in which millions of galaxies rest in a small corner, disappears when you open your eyelids?

22. O prince, I will elaborate further. Unless the knots of ignorance are cut asunder, bliss cannot be realized.

23. Failing to recognize the self is the cause of illusion. There are innumerable knots of ignorance.

24. Seeing something different from the self is the first knot

of ignorance. Those who identify their bodies with the self are ignorant. They go through the constant flux of misery and the cycles of births and deaths.

25. The second knot is seeing a distinction between the self and the world. The world is like a mirror on which reflections are made.

26-27. Seeing a difference between individuals and God is another knot. This ignorance regarding the self existed from the very beginning. It became tangled many times and has become a very complicated knot. It is with this knot that individuals are bound. Cutting this knot asunder is called liberation.

28. The perfection you attained after closing your eyes is an aspect of your own self, which remains after denying the existence of all material objects.

29. This is the infinite mirror in which the entire phenomenal world is reflected. Tell me in which objects, gross or subtle, that self does not exist?

30-31. As a barren woman cannot have a son, similarly, the real self can never be absent in an object. Without a mirror there cannot be a reflection, and without the light of *ātman*, all this would be unreal.

32. Therefore, without self-existent reality, nothing can exist. In such a state, it does not make any difference whether you open or close your eyes.

33. If one believes that there is a particular method for attaining the self, that belief itself is a knot. As long as the feeling that "I know reality through a particular method" remains, you have not attained reality, because anything that can be achieved through any method is not the Absolute.

34. What you believe you have attained by closing your eyes cannot be the ultimate, because its perfection is marred by the process itself.

35. Supreme knowledge is like an omnipotent and omniscient

fire that consumes all illusions. All mental impurities are burnt by the fire of knowledge. After realizing that state, nothing more remains to be attained.

36-37. After cutting this knot asunder, one has perfect mastery over the mind and its modifications. See the blissful, all-pervading *ātman*. See the entire reflection of the universe in the mirror of the *ātman* within you.

38. Do not ever contemplate that "All this is *ātman*." Rather, transcend and become established in the experience of *ātman* itself.'

39. Hearing his wife, Hemacūḍa's mind became completely purified. After seeing the perfect self everywhere, all his confusion vanished.

40-42. Step by step, with his firm faith, he attained maturity in his realization and became firm in that consummate state. After that he lived for several years as a *jīvanmukta,* liberated here and now, while enjoying worldly pleasures, conquering enemies, amassing wealth, and performing elaborate religious ceremonies and rituals.

43-44. Seeing this state, both his father, Muktacūḍa, and his uncle, Maṇicūḍa, wondered, 'Why is Hemacūḍa not as before? He is neither exhilarated by pleasures nor affected by pain.

45. How did he establish himself in the self by attaining tranquility? These days he takes care of the entire administration like an actor on a stage.

46. He is overwhelmed with bliss all the time. He performs his duties conscientiously, yet it seems as though his mind is firmly established in the self.

47. How did this happen?' Curious, they approached Hemacūḍa one day and asked, 'How did you attain this state of self-illumination?'

48-53. He explained the whole story and, hearing that, his father and uncle also became enlightened. After that, the king's ministers also were liberated. In this way everyone in that great city, even the children and cowherds, learned the method of attaining bliss. Men and women, young and old, after learning about pure consciousness and the universe, transcended their egos and body awareness. By having control over their emotions, they performed their worldly duties.

54-55. Mothers fed their children while discussing the absolute reality. Servants would talk about truth as they worked, and actors performed dramas with spiritual themes.

56. Musicians composed songs of spiritual wisdom, and comedians entertained their audiences, making them aware through comedy that the world in which they live is false.

57. Teachers presented scriptures full of spiritual examples in order to strengthen the zeal of their students.

58. In that great city men, women, servants, actors, clowns, soldiers, laborers, architects, and courtesans all realized the ultimate goal.

59-61. Although they continued their occupations as determined by their previous *saṁskāras,* they never considered their given duties to be good or bad, auspicious or inauspicious. They bothered themselves neither about the past nor the future and thus remained cheerful by living in the present, overwhelmed with bliss while discharging their duties.

62. The seer Śaṅkha and other *ṛṣis* once came to that city and named it Vidyānagara, the City of Wisdom.

63. Parrots and cockatoos in their cages sang the song of eternal wisdom. 'Contemplate the self as pure consciousness, beyond both subject and object.

64. Like reflections in a mirror, this external world is not different from consciousness. I am consciousness, and consciousness is immovable, yet it makes other objects move.

65-68. O people of the world, end your ignorance by fixing your awareness one-pointedly on ever-illumined consciousness. Meditate on that which is the source of all.'

This illustrious city where even the birds spoke wisely still exists today. Thus, in ancient times, King Hemacūḍa received knowledge from Hemalekhā and lived as a knower of truth and a liberated being. Through him all the men, women, and children of that region realized the absolute truth."

69. Dattātreya continued his teaching to Paraśurāma: "Therefore *satsaṅga,* the company of sages, is the first step in attaining the highest goal. One who aspires to attain the ultimate should seek the company of the saints."

Thus ends Chapter 10, with the analysis and knowledge of ātman.

11

The Nature of the Universe Is Explained

1. AFTER LISTENING to the wonderful story of Hemalekhā, Paraśurāma still had some doubts and continued asking,

2. "*Gurudeva!* The wondrous knowledge that you have imparted is amazing. It is difficult, almost impossible, to comprehend.

3. How can this external world be just consciousness? I do not perceive it that way. I can accept your claim on faith, but not through any other means.

4-5. I cannot experience consciousness without an object. It is not logical. How can I assimilate this? Kindly explain this to me." Dattātreya replied,

6. "O Paraśurāma, I will reveal the secret of the existence of the external world. This entire universe exists only in the eyes of the perceiver. It has no existence of its own.

7. I will tell you the way. Listen carefully. These objects are said to be effects, having a cause behind them.

8. Anything that appears in a new form is called birth. The universe changes its form all the time. That's why it always looks totally different.

9. Some learned people believe that objects are born every

moment, while others consider the external world to be a combination of basic elements.

10. However, all these viewpoints conclude that this universe is a product. We cannot believe that this universe is produced without any efficient cause, because it cannot be produced without consciousness.

11. Through the syllogism called *anvaya vyatireka,* the universal relationship between cause and effect can be determined. Therefore, the world could not come into existence without its cause.

12. Sometimes the cause of an effect is not apparent. In that case, one can imagine it. This is a valid inference and has been confirmed by the wise.

13-14. Generally, an effect is preceded by a cause. If the cause is not seen, then one should infer the cause, as one does in other cases. Otherwise the universal relationship between cause and effect would be contradictory. Whenever people want to do something, they start collecting equipment and preparing materials for it. Therefore, all the objects have their cause.

15-16. Some believe that the universe is a production of atoms, which, being invisible and insentient, are almost non-existent. Although the material world evolves from those atoms, this is entirely different from non-existence. Co-existence of real and unreal is self-contradictory.

17-18. That which is not yellow cannot be yellow, and light cannot be dark, because the two contradict each other. If this principle is denied, the statement will be full of defects. Even through the will of God, how can activity arise in primordial nature, which is unconscious?

19-20. Therefore, in the beginning of creation, *prakṛti,* the primordial cause from which this entire universe evolves, consists of three basic but unconscious aspects. Yet one never sees any action occurring in the unconscious principle without conscious direction. In this way the cause of the universe remains unseen, and for determining the nature of that unseen cause, the sayings of the Vedas alone furnish evidence.

21-23. The individual perceiver is imperfect; so, other than authoritative testimony, nothing can inform us of that unseen cause. An effect is never found without a cause. Therefore this universe is the work of some doer, and that doer must be pure consciousness. The universe is a stupendous effect, beyond all human comprehension. That power beyond comprehension is complete, and the Vedas explain it. That self-existent reality is explained by the Vedas beyond all doubts.

24-27. Lord Maheśvara existed before creation. He is perfectly independent; without using any object or means or materials, Maheśvara, on his own, created a canvas and painted on it. That is what the universe is. While dreaming, a person creates an entire dream world in his mind and identifies with his dream body. Yet, when he awakens, his dream body vanishes. Similarly, at the time of annihilation, the world dissolves. But the self-existent reality remains as it is.

28. As your body is different from your consciousness, similarly, the world is different from self-existent pure consciousness. He projected this universe on himself. This is all That.

29. When there is only one reality, then how can this universe be projected? There cannot be two existences.

30. By denying consciousness, even the existence of time and space cannot be proven. Through what means can one prove the absence of consciousness? Consciousness is certainly the highest reality.

31-33. Reality is ever-illumined and underlies the entire universe of name and form. Waves cannot exist without the ocean, nor light without the sun, nor can the universe exist without the substratum of consciousness. At the beginning of creation there was Maheśvara, the pure supreme consciousness. This entire universe is born from him, is maintained in him, and finally dissolves into him.

34. This theory is supported by the *āgamas,* the revealed scriptures. There can be no question about its validity. Whenever a doubt about the unseen and unknown arises, the sayings alone furnish evidence.

35. There are certain unusual powers, attained through mantras and gems. The power of mantras and gems cannot be comprehended by individuals with limited knowledge. Likewise, the scriptures' descriptions of the supreme reality and the path to attaining it must be valid, even though they are sometimes difficult to understand.

36. Therefore the *āgamas* revealed by Maheśvara are the greatest and most reliable source of knowledge related to the absolute reality. In those scriptures it is said that before the manifestation of the universe, the Lord alone existed in his glory.

37-38. He manifested the universe without anyone's help because he is perfect, pure, and sovereign. He projects the universe on his own screen of consciousness. The universe cannot exist outside of him.

39. Because the supreme being is all-pervading, nothing remains apart from him—for anything beyond the pale of consciousness could never be known to exist.

40. If you accept that the universe appears in the supreme being, like a reflection exists in a mirror, then all problems are solved.

41. The manifestation of the universe is like the action of a yogi that created this universe with his willpower.

42-43. O Paraśurāma, your fantasies are purely imaginary, yet even in those, many unique and worldly objects appear and disappear. But actually, everything in your imagination is only the projection of your mind. All that appears and disappears does so within the mind.

44-45. Just as imaginary objects have the quality of the mind, so things appearing from Maheśvara, the supreme consciousness, share his nature. Pure consciousness has no physical or visible body. Tripurā is identical to pure consciousness. Infinite power is her essential nature. She is perfect and without limitation and witnesses the whole universe.

46-47. Time and space are the limiting conditions of this manifest world. Space is identical to form, and time is identical to action. Dependent as these are on pure consciousness, how can space and time limit consciousness?

48. Tell me of a time and place which is not permeated by consciousness. Without a substratum of consciousness, how can time and space be known? Therefore, consciousness alone exists.

49. The essence of all things that can be indicated by words is nothing but spiritual illumination. Spiritual illumination and consciousness are one. Without self-illumination, nothing can be known. Therefore, illuminate thyself.

50. Only that light (knowledge) is supreme which is self-illumined and not dependent on any other means. Unconscious objects (like the fire, the sun, or the moon) are not self-luminous because they are dependent on their source, which is Maheśvara.

51. Consciousness is self-effulgent. Unconscious objects can be known against the background of consciousness.

52. If you say that objects exist even when they are not in that light, then listen. In that case there would be no consistency in determining the existence or non-existence of objects.

53-54. As reflections have no existence of their own, so, also, objects of the world have no existence of their own. As images are seen in the mirror, so the universe is an image in the mirror of consciousness. In reality, consciousness is everything. That which is seen here, there, and everywhere in all forms is the glory and greatness of that power.

55-57. A reflection is caused by the clarity of the mirror's surface. Note the difference in the reflections which appear in a clean mirror and in clear, still water. Because a mirror is unconscious and does not have freedom of will, it requires an object to reflect. However, consciousness is pure and free and does not depend on an external object. Purity of consciousness needs no evidence. The appearance of many in reality is impurity.

58-60. Multiplicity is diversity and is not found in unitary and indivisible consciousness. Objects that do not really exist, but appear to exist, are all hallucinations. The entire universe is an illusion.

61-62. The universe does not appear by itself; it appears as it is because of the self-illumined existent reality behind it. The mind projects all the colors. Just as the images in the mirror are not any part of the mirror, so the universe and its images are not any aspect of consciousness.

63-64. Just as reflection is inseparable from a mirror, this entire reflected universe is inseparable from consciousness. A mirror cannot produce an image without an object, but consciousness does not need an object to manifest itself.

65. Look at your own experience, O Paraśurāma. How many images can be projected on the screen of your mind?

66. *Saṅkalpa śakti,* the power of determination, is a prerequisite for attaining pure consciousness. Without *saṅkalpa śakti,* or firm determination, the seeker is unable to attain pure consciousness.

67-68. This universe was manifested by absolute, self-existent reality using *saṅkalpa śakti* as its instrument. The world is an image of absolute consciousness that appears on the background of consciousness. That is why it lasts for a long time.

69. The power of consciousness is perfect because the will of the absolute determined its manifestation independently. In the case of human beings, the will remains distracted.

70. But with the help of gems, mantra, and spiritual practice, the power of sovereignty expands and the limitations of experience are minimized.

71. O Paraśurāma, as a magician creates illusory objects for his audience, similarly the objects of the world are illusory, created by self-existent reality.

72. The illusions he wills into existence are seen by all, seem permanent, tangible, and can be used like gross objects; he then assimilates them. This is the case with the universe.

73. Look at the objects created by the mental power of a yogi. They are stable even though the yogi's powers are limited. Things created by the yogi appear only outside his body.

74-75. Consciousness is infinite; therefore, the universe is enveloped by the power of consciousness. All else is fancy. Only through discrimination, and not by any other means, can one cut the knots of illusion.

76. Truth is unchanging, while untruth is constantly changing. Constant change is the nature of the universe.

77. Discriminate between that which is ever-changing and that which is changeless. The world comprises both. Know this.

78-79. The ever-changing image in the mirror is impermanent, but consciousness is everlasting and changeless. That which constantly changes cannot be analyzed. As the owl is blinded by the sunlight, so ignorance disappears if the right analysis is done.

80-81 That which is food for one is poison for another. That which is divine for yogis is not divine for the ignorant.

82-84. All the images reflected in the mirror are images and thus unreal. The universe is like a mirror; consciousness, seen through it, creates hallucinations. If the world is examined with the faculty of discrimination, it is seen to be illusory.

85. Tripurā, the great majesty, shines everywhere. In this way, pure consciousness and the identity of the universe have been explained systematically."

Thus ends Chapter 11, with the explanation of consciousness and the nature of the universe.

12

The Immense Powers of Yoga

1. AFTER LISTENING TO THE NATURE of the universe as Dattātreya described it, Paraśurāma's mind was still filled with doubts. He asked,

2. "Lord, I have listened to your ideas about the universe. Whatever you say must be true.

3. Nevertheless, I do not understand why this universe appears to be real. Why have so many wise people decided it does, in fact, exist?

4. Why does this universe seem to be real, though you say it is unreal? Kindly teach me how the universe is unreal by removing my doubts."

5-6. The great sage then began to explain why the universe is mistaken as real.

"Listen, Paraśurāma. This illusion is ancient and rooted in ignorance, which causes one thing to be mistaken for another.

7. The real self is ignored because one identifies oneself with the body. Here we find flesh, blood, and bones on one side and pure consciousness (*ātman*) on the other. There is a vast difference between the perishable and imperishable.

8. It is a deep-rooted habit of human beings to identify the

body with consciousness. Consciousness is pure and unblemished.

9. This universe also appears to be real because of identification. By changing one's deep-rooted habit of identifying the self with the body, this false concept must be removed.

10. The universe will appear to be the way one believes it to be. The yogis with their contemplation and meditation identify themselves with *ātman.*

11. In this regard, let me relate a wonderful story. In the country of Baṅga there is a holy city named Sundarapura.

12. There was a wise king named Suṣeṇa. His younger brother, Mahāsena, loved him very much.

13. Suṣeṇa ruled his kingdom righteously and was highly respected. One day he decided to worship Lord Śiva through the *aśvamedha* ceremony.

14. His powerful sons and huge army accompanied the ritual horse. The princes defeated all the warriors who tried to capture the horse.

15-16. Following the horse, they arrived at the bank of the Iravati River. There they passed the hermitage of the sage Taṅgaṇa. The arrogant soldiers ignored the sage and passed without paying homage to him.

17. Taṅgaṇa's son became enraged at this slight to his father. He captured the horse and the princes who were guarding the horse.

18-19. The princes and their army surrounded the horse, but suddenly the young man took the animal and entered into the side of the rock-like mountain, while the princes watched in astonishment.

20. When they saw the young ascetic entering the rock, they attacked it with their weapons and broke the rock.

21-23. The young yogi emerged from behind the broken rock with a huge army and rapidly conquered the opposing army, captured the princes, and took the army inside the rocky mountain. The soldiers who escaped reported to the king. Suṣeṇa was amazed to hear this story and spoke to his younger brother.

24. 'Mahāsena, go to that hermitage where the sage Taṅgaṇa resides. These yogis have immense powers. They cannot be defeated even by gods.

25. Be humble, please the yogis, and bring back the horse and my sons. But it should be done immediately so that the time of ritual does not pass.

26. Do not be egotistical in front of the yogis. If they get angry, they can curse you and convert you into ashes with their yogic power.

27. Accomplish your mission respectfully so that our purpose will be fulfilled.' Thus commanded by the king, Mahāsena left for the ashram.

28. There he saw the sage Taṅgaṇa sitting in his hermitage, still in meditation. His body was still, like a log of wood, and steady, like a wall; his senses and mind were tranquil.

29-30. His ego was fully dissolved in the ocean of bliss. Mahāsena prostrated in front of him with folded hands and started singing the praise of the sage. For three days, he prayed to the sage with reverence.

31-32. The son was pleased with this praise of his father. He approached Mahāsena and said, 'I am pleased with the respect you have given my father. Tell me, how can I help you? I am the son of the sage Taṅgaṇa.

33-34. My father is in deep *samādhi* and will come out after completing twelve years. Only five years have passed, so he has to complete another seven years.

35-38. Whatever you desire, you will get. Do not think of me as a child. Like my father, I am also a yogi, and nothing is impossible for a yogi.'

Listening to the young yogi, the wise Mahāsena paid homage

with folded hands. 'O young sage, if you really want to help me, I would like to see your father when he comes out of *samādhi*. This is my earnest desire.

39. If you think that I deserve your blessing, please fulfill this desire.' The young yogi replied,

40-41. 'O prince, by no means will it be possible to fulfill your desire. However, I will do whatever I can for you. Wait for a moment and I will demonstrate my yogic power.

42. At this moment, my father is established in perfect peace. Who can wake him up from deep *samādhi?* I will try to find a method that will bring him out of *samādhi*.'

43-46. He sat down and started to pay attention to the flow of his breath. In moments, he became motionless. With his one-pointed mind, he contacted the sage. At that moment, the sage opened his eyes.

47. Calmly and cheerfully, he said, 'Son, do not commit this mistake again. Anger is the enemy of meditation.

48. It is customary for a king to always protect the yogis. Do not disturb the king's rituals.

49. Therefore, be happy and return the horse immediately so that the time of the ceremony does not expire.' Thus, he persuaded his son to immediately return the horse and the princes so that the ceremony could be performed at the appointed time.

50. Calmed by his father and following his command, the young sage went into the hill of rock and returned with the horse and the princes and handed them over to Mahāsena.

51-53. Mahāsena sent his kinsmen and the horse back to the capital. Then he once more paid homage to Taṅgaṇa and respectfully inquired, 'Lord, I cannot understand how my nephews and the horse could live inside a rock. Please explain this to me.'

54-56. Taṅgaṇa replied, 'Prince, listen to my story. Once upon a time, I myself was a king and ruled a country surrounded by the ocean. With the grace of the supreme being, I attained knowledge of Tripurā, the mother of the universe, whose nature is pure consciousness. After realizing the mystery of Tripurā, the objects of the world lost their charm and value for me. Thus, disinterested in worldly activities, I turned over my kingdom to my sons, and retired into this forest. My devoted wife accompanied me.

57-58. For thousands of years, I have done my austerities. While serving me, my wife also attained the highest goal of life. Once, under the influence of some *saṁskāras,* the mind of my wife, who was ever devoted to me alone, became sexually aroused while she was in meditation.

59-60. She saw I was in deep meditation, but could not control her urge. She had a deep desire and she became pregnant and gave birth to a self-illumined son.

61. She woke me up and put the son on my lap. Dropping her body, she left for her celestial abode.

62. I saw the child in my lap and realized that my wife had died. I raised the child with great care and love.

63. One day, my son learned about my past and the way I had ruled a kingdom. He also wanted to be a king and requested me to help him. I initiated him into the science and philosophy of yoga.

64-65. Following my instructions, he attained the highest yogic state. Then through his *saṅkalpa śakti,* the power of determination, he created a universe in this rock, where he rules a continent surrounded by an ocean. It was to that world that he took your nephews and the horse he has just released.

66. In this way I have explained their imprisonment in the hill.' Having listened to the sage, Mahāsena asked further,

67. 'I have heard this wonderful story from you personally. I want to see that wonderful place. Can you comply with my request?'

68. After Mahāsena prayed to the sage, the sage ordered his son to show him all of his creation.

69-70. Having thus instructed his son, the sage again went to the depths of *samādhi.* Then the young yogi led Mahāsena to the hill and entered it, but the prince could not follow. He called to the young yogi.

71. From inside the hill, the young yogi called back to the prince, and then came out and said,

72. 'You are not a yogi. That is why you are having difficulty entering the hill. Because you do not have yogic powers, this is a difficult task for you.

73-74. Drop your gross body in this hole. Then you will have access.' But the prince could not do so. The prince said,

75. 'O yogi, tell me how to consciously drop my body. I will die if I leave it forcibly.'

76. The young sage smilingly said, 'You do not know yoga science. Close your eyes.'

77. The prince gently closed his eyes and the young yogi entered his body, and pulling the subtle body out, left the physical body in the pit.

78. Then, by using his yogic power, he entered the hill, taking the prince with him.

[*Note: The yogi here demonstrates parakāyā praveśa vijñāna. This is a rare technique known only by the highly accomplished adepts.*]

79. Jolted by this separation from his physical body, Mahāsena's subtle body lost consciousness. The young sage united the prince's subtle body with a gross body he materialized through his *saṅkalpa śakti,* and the prince regained consciousness. He realized the young sage was transporting him across a vast abyss. Above, below, and to all sides he saw infinite, bewildering space.

80-82. Terrified, he cried, 'O great sage, forsake me not. If I am lost in this limitless space, I will die.' The young sage laughed at his fear and gave him courage. 'This is the world inside the hill. Look around fearlessly.'

83-86. Having regained his courage, Mahāsena saw different planets in the distance, surrounded by darkness. He moved to that region of remote planets, looked down, and saw a large moon. He moved to the moon but nearly froze because the moon was so cold. Fortunately, the young sage protected him. He then moved to a planet where he found himself scorched by the rays of the sun. The young sage comforted him with the help of yogic power. All the planets seemed to him like reflections of paradise.

87-90. Then he landed in the peaks of the Himalayas with the yogi. From there he could see all the sites the sage pointed out, for the yogi gave him powerful eyesight so that he could see continents at great distances. He saw a ring-like mountain named Lokāloka. Beyond that was a golden land. He also saw oceans, rivers, seven different continents covered with mountains, bright beings, demons, men, primitive tribes, and semi-humans like *yakṣas* and *kinnaras.*

91-95. He also saw the young sage himself residing in the form of Brahmā, Viṣṇu, and Śiva, living in Satyaloka, Vaikuṇṭha, and Kailāsa, respectively. Mahāsena also saw that, at the same time, the young sage had taken another form and was ruling the earth as its emperor. He was amazed by this great yogic power of the young sage. The young sage told him, 'O prince, twelve thousand years have passed while we have been visiting this world. Now we will return to the outside world where my father resides.'

96. Having said this, he returned to the world with the prince. He came out of the hill as he had entered.

Thus ends Chapter 12, which explains a few yogic powers.

13

The Young Yogi Imparts the Knowledge of *Ātman* to the Grieving Mahāsena

1-2. AFTER COMING OUT OF THE HILL, the young sage made the prince's subtle body unconscious, drew it out of the body he had materialized for him, and united it with his original physical body. Then he restored his awareness to the former world.

3-4. After awakening, Mahāsena saw his former world and was surprised to see the earth, men, trees, streams, and lakes in completely different forms. He asked, 'O great one, what is this new world you are showing me now?

5-6. Here is still another universe. How wonderful it is.'

The young yogi replied, 'O prince, this is the same country where we lived before. A long time has passed. That is why it seems fresh and new.

7-8. We spent one day in the world which exists inside the rock, while here in the world outside, twelve thousand years have passed. That is why this world seems so different. There are differences in the way people live and their behavior. Their languages are totally different.

9. People go through such changes with the passage of time. I have seen this sort of thing many times.

10. See right over there, my almighty father is still in *samādhi.* This is the very place where you praised him with great honor.

11. In front of you is the huge rock which we entered. Inside that rock you saw a new world created through yogic powers. During that period, thousands of years have passed.

12. In your country of Baṅga, where the beautiful capital, Sundarapura, existed, there is a thick, huge forest where jackals and other animals live.

13. Vīrabāhu comes from your brother's lineage. His capital, Viśālā, in the state of Malava, is situated on the bank of the Kṣiprā River.

14. There is another king, Suśarmā, descended from him who rules the Draviḍa country, living in the city of Varddhana near the Tāmraparṇī River.

15. Such is the state of the world, which is ever-changing. In a few moments, a completely new world appears.

16. After many, many years, these mountains, rivers, lakes, and the earth itself will change. Change is the habit of the world.

17-18. Lowlands rise, mountains crumble into pits, and deserts become tropical. Rocky land becomes sandy, and sandy land turns rocky.

19. Infertile land becomes fertile, and lush land, infertile. Gems turn into pebbles, and pebbles into precious gems.

20. Fresh water becomes salty, and salt water, sweet. Countries inhabited by men become havens for animals.

21. There was a time when the earth was inhabited primarily by insects and worms. Thus, in the course of time, the world changes.

22. These changes occur on earth in the course of time. In fact, the earth remains the same.'

Deeply grieved, Mahāsena fainted.

23-26. Revived by the yogi, he plunged into grief and started mourning for his wife, brother, and children. The young sage consoled him with his wisdom. 'O prince, you are a brilliant man. Why do you mourn?

27. A wise man never does anything without a purpose. One who performs an action without knowing its consequence is a fool.

28-29. Now tell me the cause of your grief and how it will serve you.' Mahāsena replied with great anguish, 'O sage, can you not see the cause of my grief? Even knowing that I have just lost everything, you are asking this question?

30. A person who loses just one family member is overcome with grief. But I have lost my whole family and my kingdom. And still you're asking why I'm sad.'

31-32. The sage, laughing, asked, 'Prince, is it your family tradition to believe that if you do not grieve, a great misfortune will befall you? Do you think that by lamenting, those lost things will be regained?

33-34. Have courage and know that by grieving, nothing is achieved. If you think it is necessary to grieve for lost relatives, then you should continue grieving your whole life for your grandfather and many other older relatives who have died. Why do you not express your grief for them also?

35-36. Whose relatives were they, actually? How did they become your relatives? In your parents' stool and even in your own, there are millions of worms. They are also born from and related to your body. Why do you not consider them your relatives and grieve for them, also?

37. Prince, remember who you really are. Why this sorrow? Are you the body, or are you different from it? The body is composed of many elements.

38-40. That which is called destruction, is it of all parts or just one? Parts of the body are being destroyed at every moment. For example, urine, feces, mucus, nails, and hair are being excreted continually, while the body still exists. Earth, water, and the other elements are the constituents of your brother's physical body. These elements still exist.

41. You are not actually the body, although you have a body. Just as you say that these are "my garments," you also say "this is my body." Can you explain how you and the body are one and the same? They are not.

42-43. Don't have doubt regarding this. What relationship do you establish between yourself and another body? Do you ever find yourself attached to your brother's garments? Why then mourn for the dead, which are exactly like garments. Prince, tell me, when you refer to "my body," "my senses," "my *prāṇa,*" and "my mind," can you tell me who you are?'

44-46. Mahāsena started pondering this puzzle. He wanted to solve it, and when he could not find the answer, he again became sad and humbly said, 'Lord, I do not really know who I am. Without knowing the exact reason, out of habit, I am feeling sad. I am helpless. I surrender myself at your feet. Lord, what is the secret?

47. When someone dies, his relatives grieve. They do not know their essential nature, yet they grieve.

48. Lord, I submit myself to you. Please accept me as your disciple. Please explain this whole thing to me.'

Hearing this, the sage's son spoke,

49-52. 'Listen, Mahāsena. People deluded by the illusory power of the great goddess do not realize their essential nature and grieve uselessly. As long as they do not realize the *ātman,* they are overcome by sorrow. After realization one no longer grieves, just as one forgets his dream identity and concerns when he awakens.

53-54. After the dreamer awakens or an audience understands how a trick was performed, their reaction to the dream or illusion disappears. In fact, they laugh at themselves for having been deluded. Likewise, a person who has realized the self and crossed the mire of delusion feels compassion for pitiful people like you.

55. After realizing the self, one can cross the ocean of sorrow. O mighty prince, realize the *ātman,* and cast off this sorrow created by delusion.'

56. Mahāsena said, 'Lord, the example of dreams and magic does not seem to be appropriate.

57-58. The objects created in a dream or through magic simply appear and do not serve any purpose, but objects of the waking state seem to be real and useful. They are perfectly tangible, not unreal at all. How can they be the same as dream objects?'

The young yogi responded,

59. 'Prince, listen. What you said about my example not fitting is another example of misunderstanding. You are as doubly confused as a person confused in a dream.

60. A dream tree serves a purpose in the dream. Is it possible for the travelers to rest under the tree?

61. As dreamers are satisfied during dreaming, those who are awake cannot enjoy the fruits of their dreams. Does not the fruit of that tree satisfy the dreamer?

62. If you say that dream objects lose their existence the moment a person awakens, wait. Is it not also true that objects corresponding to the waking state vanish in deep sleep?

63. If you claim that when you wake up the objects that were there yesterday are still there today, then tell me if it is not true that dream objects can also be re-experienced.

64. If you say that in a dream there is no recurrence of dream experience and, consequently, the objects of the dream are unreal, then listen. Where is the recurrence of a given object in the waking state, since objects in the waking state also change?

65-67. Are you suggesting that the mountains, ocean, and earth—all these forms which we see—really exist permanently? In fact, they are constantly changing. The dream world experiences are similar. In dreams, the earth, mountains, rivers, friends, and relatives are experienced exactly the way they are experienced in the waking state.

68. Mountains and other objects of the world also change if you see them again. How can they be real? In the summer there are no waterfalls, but in the rainy season they appear.

69. Similarly, animals, insects, thunder, clouds, lightning, and storms constantly change. Similar changes occur on the earth and in the ocean.

70. Even the oceans are constantly changing. I am telling you—try to think at a more subtle level.

71-72. Objects in both dreaming and waking states are constantly subject to change. However, in practical life, there is obviously some difference. In the waking state, the objects experienced are similar to the objects experienced in the dreaming state. Their fundamental continuity cannot be ignored.

73-74. If you consider dreams illusory, I want to know what illusion is. Illusion depends on the appearance and disappearance of objects from our senses.

75-76. Everything vanishes in deep sleep. Those who do not have clear insight into the nature of the objects cannot prove the validity of any object, because of their distorted minds.

77. This world is similar to the world experienced in the dream state. Dreams can also be prolonged.

78. As long as the dream persists, its objects appear real. They serve the intended purpose of the dream and appear perfectly stable. Objects in the external world corresponding to the waking state have exactly the same property.

79. Just as a person is aware of the waking state when he is awake, in the same way, in the dream state he is aware of dream objects.

80. Prince, if the waking and dream states are similar, why does one not mourn for relatives lost in the dreaming state?

81. The reality of the external world is a projection of one's

mind. If someone thinks it is unreal, then, for that person, this universe certainly becomes unreal.

82. We have promoted the idea that this universe is real because we have not even considered that alternative. Prince, after realizing *ātman* you will know that everything I am saying is true.

83. The world you just experienced is an example of my statements. If you want to experience it again, let us go to the hill once more and circumambulate it.'

84-86. The son of the sage took the prince around the huge rocky hill, saying, 'Prince, this whole rocky hill is just one mile around, but you saw the entire universe in it. Was it false or true? Was it a dream or was it real?

87. One day in the world inside the rock is experienced as twelve thousand years outside. Now decide which universe is more real.

88. Like two different dreams, you cannot explain one in terms of the other. The obvious conclusion is that the whole universe is one's own imagination.

89. Without this imagination, it would disappear instantly. Therefore, console yourself. The world is like a dream. Do not mourn the death of your brother.

90. The mind is like a canvas on which the various objects of the universe appear to be painted. Those objects are similar, like images seen in the mirror. So be free from depression caused by the death of relatives in the dreaming state.

91. O prince, realize that the self is manifesting itself in the world. The self is pure and supreme consciousness. Realizing this, experience the happiness within.'

Thus ends Chapter 13, in which the simile of the interior of the mountain of rock is explained from the yogic viewpoint.

14

Saṅkalpa Śakti and the Way to Attain It

1. AFTER LISTENING TO THE SAGE'S SON with his purified mind, Mahāsena started seeing things more clearly. Comparing the objects of the external world with the objects seen in the dreaming state, he attained freedom from sorrow.

2. With courage and freedom from sorrow, he asked the son of the sage, 'O great wise one, you can see beyond. You have profound knowledge and know that which can be known through the sense and that which the senses cannot reach.

3-4. However, still there is something I do not understand. Kindly answer my questions. You said that all this happened through imagination. How? No matter how much I imagine something, it does not necessarily occur outside me.

5. Because your willful thinking is perfected, you could materialize a whole universe inside a hill. This external world and the hill world co-exist. Why then are there differences between time and space in the two worlds?

6. Surely one of them must be unreal. Which is it?'

The yogi replied,

7. 'Here "imagination" is identical with "determination," which is of two kinds: perfect and imperfect. Imagination

without doubt is helpful. The absence of doubt means the continuity of one thought.

8. The universe is in existence because of the desire of Brahmā, the creator. Brahmā created the universe with his powerful desire.

9. The world created by your desire and will was not created with determination and will, like the creation of Brahmā.

10-11. O prince, there are varieties of *siddhis.* One is by birth; the second is by obtaining a jewel; the third is through herbs; the fourth is through yoga *sādhanā;* the fifth is through austerities; the sixth is through mantra; and the seventh is through a boon.

12. Brahmā received that power by birth; *yakṣas* and demons, through gems; *devas,* through herbs; yogis, through yoga; austere people, through austerity; mantra adepts, through mantra; and the celestial architect, Viśvakarmā, through a boon.

13-14. By self-determination, the past *saṅkalpas* are forgotten. *Saṅkalpa* should be done with full determination.

15. One should wash off all those old stains of the mind in order to make new and effective disciplines. Such a one-pointed concept cannot be obstructed in any way. All great things can be achieved through such a power.

16. Your mind is not one-pointed and concentrated. Therefore you should learn to focus your mind.

17. O prince, let me explain the secret of time and space.

18. This seems to be an amazing mystery to you because you are not an adept. I can explain it clearly. It is the nature of the universe to appear in diverse forms.

19. Light is one thing, yet it is experienced in two ways. For creatures, like owls, who are blind during the day, it appears in the form of darkness, while for others it takes the form of light.

20. Men and animals drown in water, while fish suffocate in air.

21-22. Fire burns men and other creatures, but the *tittira,* a legendary bird, swallows fire. Fire is extinguished by water, but flames thrive on oil.

23. Thus, hundreds and thousands of objects are contrary to each other. Listen carefully, and I will tell you the reason.

24-25. Sight cannot exist without the eye. A diseased eye, like one afflicted with myopia, creates double vision.

26-32. Unusual vision is the product of diseased eyes. As eye diseases can be cured by proper treatment, similarly, the mind's impurities can be removed by right *sādhanā.*

In the eastern island of Karaṇḍaka, red is seen all the time. Everything is seen upside down on the island of Ramaṇaka. In the same way, on other islands, people perceive things differently according to their vision. If anyone sees things differently than his peers, he tries to cure what he considers to be his visual problem so he can see in the same way everyone else does.

Whatever one sees in the world depends on the vision of the eye. In the same manner smell, taste, sound, and tactile sensation exist only in their corresponding senses. All mental impressions are merely part of the mind. Time and space arise in the mental horizon. The relationship between time, space, and objects is according to your estimate of them.

33. Prince, listen. The inner reality is actually the cause of the universe. As the mirror supports the image, the universe is supported by the self-existent reality.

34-37. The body is an external sheath. But how can it be excluded from its inner dweller? As the pot is different from the pot maker, so the body is different from the soul. The body is different from the seer. That which is seen is seen because of illumination. In the absence of that, nothing can be seen. Actually, all the illumined objects are within the vision of the seer. The seer and the seen are not one and the same.

38-40. The body or mind cannot be the seer because, like mountains and other objects, they are seen by other lights. The self-illumined seer does not need to be illuminated by any source because he is the only source of all light.

41-42. Time and space are the extension of the self-illumined being. For the self-illumined existence, there is nothing like within and without. As the peak cannot be separate from the mountain, similarly, illumination cannot be separate from the self.

43-44. The whole universe is always encompassed by light within and without. Such light is transcendental and is called the supreme Tripurā, the supreme goddess. Knowers of the Vedas call her Brahman and Vaiṣṇaivites call her Viṣṇu.

45. According to *Śaivites,* she is Śiva; according to *Śaktas,* she is Śakti.

46. As the image is pervaded by the mirror, this world is pervaded by the power of consciousness. All the objects in this universe are illuminated by that light.

47-49. As the image of a city is not part of the mirror, similarly the universe is not part of consciousness. As an image cannot be separated from a mirror, the universe cannot be separated from consciousness. This is the glory of the real self.

50. Space is a void. As the world cannot be ascertained, neither can space be defined.

51. This universe dwells in the self, but the question arises: Why does consciousness assume the nature of darkness at the same time? If consciousness and brilliance are all-pervading, then from where were darkness and ignorance born?

52-53. As the mirror contains the image, so the all-pervading consciousness pervades the universe by its power. The self-existent consciousness is within and without; it is single and dense, and holds the immobile and mobile universe in its womb. Unique in its nature, it has neither motivation nor cause.

54-55. The mirror always remains unaffected. No matter how many images are reflected in it, it always retains its clarity. So is the case with self-illumined consciousness. Through his *sādhanā* an advanced meditator can verify the different states, such as waking and dreaming.'

56. The young yogi said, 'O prince, learn to examine your waking and dreaming states and the images constantly going through your mind. All these images are the products of your mind.

57. Consciousness remains unaffected before creation, after dissolution, and during the appearance of this world, as the mirror remains unaffected by the images reflected in it.

58. Though absolute, self-existent reality manifests itself, yet that self-existent reality remains unblemished by its manifestations.

59. The first step of creation was darkness. This marks the first stage of manifestation and is called *avidyā* or *tamas*. The appearance of the perfect as if it were limited or imperfect is *avidyā*.

60. The state in which absolute reality is separated from its *pūrṇāhantā*, perfect "I-am-ness," and assumes that which is contrary to perfect "I-am-ness," is called *avyakta*, the unmanifest.

61. The self-illumined consciousness is named *śiva tattva;* when it is seen externally it is called the individual feeling of "I," *śakti tattva*.

62. The externally projected *maha-śūnya*, great void, covered by *ahambhāva*, "I-am-ness," is called Sadāśiva.

63. This same *sadāśiva tattva* when dominated by unconsciousness is called Īśvara. The experience of both Sadāśiva and Īśvara, which is simultaneously dualistic and nondualistic, is called *śuddhavidyā* (pure knowledge).

64. Since thus far the objective world supported by duality has not yet emerged, this level of creation is called *śuddha*, pure creation.

65. When under the influence of *svātantrya śakti*, the experience of duality gradually expands and *jaḍaśakti* (unconsciousness) gradually dominates consciousness.

66. The insentient force is called *māyā śakti.* There is a clear difference, exactly like the difference between the seed and the sprout.

67-69. The sentient state is also called *puruṣa,* which is seated inside the five sheaths: namely, *kalā, vidyā, rāga, kāla,* and *niyati.* Limited ability to act is called *kalā;* limited power to know is called *vidyā;* desire is *rāga;* limited lifespan is *kāla;* and putting things in proper order is called *niyati.* Consciousness combined with these five limiting factors is called *puruṣa.*

70. The individual soul remains in the bondage of karma, both positive and negative, which supports the power of intelligence within and is called *prakṛti.*

71. The results of karmas are threefold—pleasant, neutral, and unpleasant. *Prakṛti* is also threefold—*sattvic, rajasic,* and *tamasic*—having the quality of light, activity, and inertia, respectively. A particular state assumed by the *citta* is called *prakṛti.*

72. That which is called *prakṛti* in the state of deep sleep is called *citta* in the waking state.

73. Because it is full of latent desires, it remains in an unmanifested state. It differs according to the individuals and their latent desires.

74. In deep sleep, all individual souls are alike. And after coming out of that state, each individual soul differs from others.

75. When consciousness is predominant, it is called *puruṣa.* When the unmanifest power is predominant, it is called *prakṛti.* According to its various functions, the same *citta* is called *ahaṅkāra, buddhi,* and mind.

76. The modifications of *citta* are ego, the faculty of discrimination, and mind. That is called *antaḥkaraṇa.*

77. From these three modifications are born five subtle senses, five gross senses, and space, wind, fire, water, and earth.

78. In this way absolute consciousness herself, the witness of all, appears as the universe, as if it were external to her.

79-80. That which is the prime cause of this universe is called

Tripurā Śakti. From its desire was born Brahmā, and from the will and determination of Brahmā this universe came into existence. But that which is "I" and "you" is pure consciousness.

81. Diversity in the universe appears because of the many phases of consciousness. When the universe dissolves, then one cannot differentiate between the real and unreal.

82. The consciousness in you is veiled by the power of maya. When that veil is lifted, consciousness shines in its glory and then *cit-śakti* shines forth.

83. According to time and space, individuals perceive objects as large, small, short, and long.

84-86. One day to me is equal to twelve thousand years of Brahmā. The space of two and one-half miles of Brahmā is infinite to me and encompasses the whole creation. Both versions have their validity.

87-88. For example, if one imagines a hill within himself and also imagines the entire universe within that hill, that concept will last as long as his imagination lasts. In the practical world, a strong willpower is important.

89. O prince, this universe reflects in the mirror of consciousness, and that which looks like the universe is an image in the mirror. The image appears in the mirror only through the power of consciousness.

90. Consciousness is like a screen, and the image is the universe. The adepts know the secrets of time and space, for they have gone beyond.

91. The yogis annihilate space in a fraction of a second and have the power of perceiving the whole universe like a seed on the palm.

92. O prince, acknowledge the fact that the universe is an image of the mirror of consciousness and concentrate with a one-pointed mind on the self. Be free from the delusion that the world is real.

93. Then you will also attain freedom as I have, by cutting

the bondage of ignorance asunder.'

94-96. Paraśurāma, by having *satsaṅga* with the sage's son the prince's ignorance was dispelled and his faculty of discrimination became sharp and purified. Finally, he knew his ultimate goal and then he practiced the technique of *samādhi*. For attaining *samādhi,* he did not depend on external crutches.

97. His life became happy and his life span was extended. He no longer identified himself with his body or any other object of the world. He became illumined and finally attained liberation.

O Paraśurāma, remember that this universe is only an image and it has no existence of its own. With the help of contemplation, doubt will be removed from your mind."

Thus ends Chapter 14, with a discussion of the nature of the real and unreal.

15

The Awareness of Consciousness and the Lesson Given to Aṣṭāvakra

1-2. PARAŚURĀMA WAS ASTONISHED by this thought-provoking story about the rocky mountain. With a purified mind he went to Dattātreya and prostrated in front of him,

3. "O lord, you imparted magnificent teachings through a story, and I began contemplating upon them.

4. I understand that pure knowledge alone is truth and that the objects of the world are as unreal as the images reflected in a mirror.

5. O Great Mother Maheśvarī, tell me if consciousness itself manifests this phenomenal world, from its unmanifested state of deep sleep to the dreaming and waking states.

6. Pure consciousness is direct knowledge. This manifestation of the universe is without any other cause, but springs spontaneously from the self-existent reality. This I understand, having listened with a purified mind.

7. Consciousness cannot be comprehended through intellectual knowledge, because it is pure and unblemished by the mind and its modifications.

8-9. I am bewildered and want to know how realization is attained, without which the goal is not attained. What is the nature of liberation? If liberation is attained in this lifetime, does the lifestyle of the liberated one change for the good? How does one behave if he is liberated?

10. The enlightened ones sometimes seem to be engaged in external activities. In such cases, how do they relate the external world to pure consciousness?

11. If they have attained the highest consciousness, how can they function in the external world? In this diversity, how can I find unity and see that liberation is possible in the midst of external activities?

12. Why do we notice apparent differences in the enlightened sages? A few seem to be active. A few are teaching the scriptures.

13. A few worship the deities in different manners. A fortunate few remain in *samādhi.*

14. Others observe austerities while mortifying their bodies and senses. A few teach their students clearly and sincerely.

15. Some of the enlightened ones rule the country with full justice. Some of them remain engaged in thrashing out philosophical differences.

16. A few of them are busy writing scriptures. Some of them pretend to be abnormal in their behavior.

17. But these individuals of different categories gain fame like the wise do.

[*Note: It is difficult for a layman to discriminate. Perfect meets perfect; for meeting perfect, one must be perfect.*]

18. How can there be a difference in their behavior if they really are liberated? Are there different states and grades of liberation?

19. Kindly resolve these conflicts, because I have immense respect for you and a burning desire to know the truth."

20. Dattātreya was pleased and answered all the questions of his favorite disciple in the following manner:

21. "Paraśurāma, you are the best among the wise. You must have had a glimpse of reality. You are endowed with good

thoughts and thus you deserve to know the truth.

22. When the mind starts treading the path of truth, then one deserves the profound grace of Mother Divine. Without her loving grace, who can attain final liberation?

23-24. The purpose is accomplished when the *sādhaka's* mind becomes joyous and he constantly contemplates and thus strengthens his creativity. So far, you have rightly understood the nature of consciousness.

25. Knowledge without profound experience is not considered to be true knowledge. Therefore, do not have any doubt.

26. The profound experience of self is constant awareness of "I am," and for such a knower the illusions of the world disappear. Indirect knowledge is like a dream.

27. As access to the treasure-house of wealth in a dream is a fantasy, so indirect knowledge is like a dream.

28. Let me explain through a beautiful story.

Once upon a time in the kingdom of Videha there was a wise king named Janaka.

29. King Janaka is always quoted as a singular example, a knower of the universe and beyond. Once he performed a ceremony for attaining final liberation.

30. Many brahmins and learned ascetics, hermits, and intellectuals well versed in the Vedas participated in the ceremony.

31. During the same time Varuṇa, the presiding deity of water, wished to perform a similar ceremony, but the prominent sages and scholars did not participate in that ceremony.

32. All the great ones from different walks of life were pleased to receive Janaka's hospitality. In revenge, Varuṇa's son persecuted many learned brahmins.

33-37. He even disguised himself as a brahmin and entered the royal house to bless the King and address the assembly, saying, 'O king, this assembly is not suitable for this occasion. It is like a beautiful lake full of lotuses being used by crows, jackdaws, and herons. These incompetent people are useless. I don't find anyone who is wise like a swan and can discriminate between truth and ignorance, as the swam separates milk from water. I do not want to participate in an assembly of idiots.'

38. Listening to these insulting words, the entire assembly of learned people became angry. 'You charlatan. What right have you to insult this assembly of wise people?

39. What ability do you have that makes you believe you can defeat us in debate? Idiot. Why are you speaking thus? You will have to debate with us before you leave this assembly.

40. Most of the educated people of the world are gathered here. You fool. Do you think you have the ability to debate with all of us?

41. Tell us what exquisite knowledge you have that will defeat us all in debate.'

To this challenge, the son of Varuṇa responded,

42-43. 'I can conquer you all in a moment, but on one condition. If you defeat me, throw me in the ocean. If I win, I will drown whomever I defeat. First accept this wager and then we will start debating.'

44. All the brahmins accepted the challenge. They debated with Varuṇa's son.

45. With his fallacious logic he defeated all of the learned people and threw them in the ocean.

46. Varuṇa's soldiers picked up the drowning people and took them to his ceremonial dais, where they were received with great reverence. Those brahmins who were drowning and then rescued were pleased by Varuṇa's hospitality.

47-50. However, Aṣṭāvakra, the son of Kahola, well versed in the art of irrational reasoning, heard of his father being thrown in the ocean. He hurried to the court and vanquished the son of Varuṇa, then ordered him to drown himself. The son of Varuṇa revealed his identity and restored the lost brahmins from his father's court. After the brahmins had been returned, Aṣṭāvakra became egotistical and boasted of his greatness. Thus insulted by

Aṣṭāvakra, the brahmins were offended.

51-52. Immediately, a woman sage arrived in saffron garb, wearing long hair like the hermits. Due to her yogic accomplishment, she looked perennially young and she was attractive. She greeted the brahmins who had taken refuge in her and after receiving due honor from the king, she consoled them and said,

53. 'O son of Kahola, indeed you are very learned. You released the brahmins by conquering Varuṇa's son in debate.

54-56. Let me ask you some questions. Answer honestly. What is that state which assures immortality? If it is known, all doubts vanish. Nothing remains unknown. Nothing remains desired, and even the unknowable becomes known. If you know it, tell me.' At this question the son of Kahola replied,

57. 'I know that state. Listen, I will tell you. There is nothing in the world I do not know, so your question is no problem for me.

58. I have studied all the branches of knowledge in depth. Whatever you ask I shall answer correctly. Just listen.

59. That truth which you asked about is actually the cause of the universe. It has no beginning, middle, or end. It is not limited by time and space. It is pure, indivisible, and eternal.

60. On the basis of that reality, this whole universe appears to exist. That truth is like a mirror which supports the image of the city which reflects in it.

61. After knowing the mirror, no doubt remains about the images reflecting in it. Similarly, after knowing that state of reality, a *sādhaka* attains immortality.

62. If one has realized the real self, nothing remains unknown. After knowing the absolute, a person desires nothing.

63. According to the scriptures, the learned sages have come to the final conclusion about the nature of the absolute reality.'

64. When he concluded, she said, 'O son of a sage, your answer is both beautiful and logical.

65. But you said no one knows that self-existent reality.

Therefore, it cannot be known. At the same time you said that only after knowing it, a *sādhaka* gains immortality.

66. Is this not a contradictory statement? If it cannot be known, then you must admit that you do not know it. Then do not say that truth does not exist.

67. But if it exists and you know it, then you cannot claim it cannot be known. Moreover, brahmin, you are making these claims on the basis of scriptural knowledge.

68-70. You do not know it directly. It is not direct knowledge. If you know about the nature of the universe and do not know the nature of the real self, what good is that knowledge? Do you not consider yourself defeated when you make such a self-contradictory statement in the court of King Janaka?' At these words, Aṣṭāvakra became mum.

71-73. He was disappointed and ashamed. Looking down, he remained silent. After seriously considering her arguments, he conceded. 'O great lady sage, I do not know the answer. I have become your disciple. Please tell me why there seem to be contradictions in the scriptures. I do not speak untruth, for it disturbs my austerities.

74. That great lady was pleased to hear that Aṣṭāvakra did not speak untruth. In front of the entire court, she told him,

75. 'Blessed son, for lack of knowing the depth of this knowledge, *sādhakas* become victims of the evil called attachment. This is not the subject matter for mere debate. The secret teaching is not fully explained by the *śāstras*.

76. In this entire assembly of the learned, no one has profound knowledge of the truth. It is known to the king and me exclusively.

77. In debates, no one raises such questions. Learned people, with the help of logic, have this knowledge in fragments.

78. Mere debate will not reveal it. One must be at the service of a great adept and blessed by the self.

79. O son of a saint, be attentive. If the mind has not attained

the state of tranquility and one-pointedness, there will be no gain.

80. Unless this profound science is fully assimilated by your inner being, your listening to the scriptures, even a thousand times, will be of no use.

81-82 If someone forgets he is wearing a necklace and presumes it has been stolen, he suffers. Even if someone tells him he is wearing it, if he does not see it, then no matter how intense his desire to find it, he will not find it.

83-84. Likewise, O son of a learned one, even after listening one-pointedly to a description of *ātman* and its nature, if one does not turn his mind inward, how can he expect to realize *ātman* within?

85-86. A lamp might shed its light around itself, but it cannot illuminate the space beneath. The sun does not depend on illumination from any other object, because the sun is self-illumined.

87-89. By judging the darkness under the lamp, you cannot doubt the existence of the light. If it is true with lamps, then what about that which can never be illumined by anything else? Someone may claim that absolute reality is ever-illumined and at the same time beyond comprehension. Think about this carefully.

90-91. Tripurā is this supreme consciousness, the source of all. Her self-existent illumination illumines all. If illumination is not her nature, then who has the power of illumination?

92. Without profound introspection, even the most learned scholars cannot comprehend this deepest knowledge. That is why throughout life they remain in the darkness of ignorance.

93. Without turning their minds inward, even great, learned men cannot fathom this mystery. That is why they remain caught in the cycle of birth and death.

94-95. Unless the mind is brought to a state of stillness, it is not possible to attain introspection. And unless introspection is fully developed, self-realization is not possible. The mind should first attain desirelessness, then it can penetrate into deeper levels.

96-97. Renounce all desires and strengthen only the one

desire that helps in self-surrender. Gain freedom. When you remember that state, then you will know that absolute reality is beyond, yet can be attained.

98. After knowing that absolute reality, you will attain the highest state of consciousness. Now I have explained all the secrets, O son of a sage. I bid goodbye to you.

99. Let me go now. By listening only once to the secret of this knowledge, you cannot know the truth. King Janaka, the wisest of the wise, will impart this knowledge to you.

100. You can ask questions to remove your doubts and the king will dispel your ignorance.'

Thus she spoke and rose from her seat. The king worshiped her, and the assembly bowed to her with great reverence.

101. She vanished suddenly, like a wind disperses the clouds."

Dattātreya said, "O Paraśurāma, I have already given you the method of realizing the self."

Thus ends Chapter 15 with the dialogue with Aṣṭāvakra on jñāna.

16

The Dialogue Between King Janaka and Sage Aṣṭāvakra

1. PARAŚURĀMA, THE SON of the great *ṛṣi* Bhṛgu, was astonished at the dialogue between sage Aṣṭāvakra and the ochre-robed *devī,* the lady renunciate. With great enthusiasm to know more, he put his question to Dattātreya:

2-3. "Lord, this ancient story is wondrous. Now kindly and systematically tell me how Aṣṭāvakra approached the great Janaka and what Janaka said. This whole story is interesting and I have never heard such a thing before.

4-5. *Gurudeva,* the subject matter of this story is the essence of all sciences. Please be kind and help me."

Thus the great sage Dattātreya began imparting the knowledge to Śrī Paraśurāma. "O Paraśurāma, listen to the tale of King Janaka attentively.

6-7. After the great lady left for her celestial abode, Aṣṭāvakra went to King Janaka, along with many brahmins. He wanted King Janaka to explain everything that was explained by the lady sage so he could assimilate it in its entirety. Listen to me with full attention.

8-9. Aṣṭāvakra said, 'The lesson that was imparted by the lady sage was very compact and abstruse. Therefore I could not assimilate it fully. Kindly tell me the way to attain that knowledge.'

King Janaka was amazed that he posed such a question.

10. 'O son of a sage, listen to me. The highest state is neither knowable nor unknowable.

11. Had it been unknowable, how could my master have taught me? The highest knowledge is imparted by the *gurudeva* alone. Therefore one should seek the refuge of a master with reverence.

12-13. Attaining that state is both very simple and very difficult. One whose mind has become one-pointed and inward, for him it is easy. One whose mind remains dissipated in the external world, for him it is very difficult.

14-15. Actually, that highest state is inexplicable and unknowable, but there is a way of knowing and attaining it. After careful analysis, the underlying principle—consciousness—is understood to be formless, abstract, and separate from the external world. Yet it illumines all the objects of the world.

16-19. That which is not self-existent reality is subject to change, and is thus unreal. Consciousness is that through which all objects of the world are known. The seen is different from the seer, otherwise it could not be seen by the seer.

Consciousness cannot be divided into parts. The division is seen in the world of objects. Their forms and names are different. Be aware of the absolute consciousness by eliminating all these fleeting forms and names.

20. As the various images are seen in the mirror, similarly pure consciousness assumes the different forms of the world.

21. Pure consciousness is the nature of the self. Therefore, it is not the subject matter of analysis.

22-23. O Aṣṭāvakra, realize yourself. Understand it. You are neither your body nor *prāṇa* nor mind, for they all are ever-changing. The body is a component of three humors—*vāta, pitta,* and *kapha.* How can they be your true nature?

24. You are not the body, senses, or mind, because they are all transient. This cannot be your true self.

25. The supreme consciousness never loses its self-awareness. Therefore, this consciousness is the knower of all.

26. Turn your eyes inward and try to realize yourself as pure consciousness. The best students glimpse their essential nature even as the teacher is describing it.

27. By eyes, I do not mean the physical eyes, but the mental eye through which one sees dreams. It is important to know that.

28. Turning the mind's eye inward means directing the mind within, because nothing internal can be seen without an inward and one-pointed mind.

29-30. When a person wants to look at something, he first withdraws his attention from everything else and contacts only the object that he wants to see. Only then does he perceive it. Without focusing his mind, he cannot see even objects directly in front of him.

31. Those who do not withdraw their attention from here and there cannot see the object in front of their eyes. O brahmin, the nature of the other senses is similar.

32-33. This applies to the mind when pain and pleasure are felt. When the mind is engaged elsewhere, pain and pleasure are not felt.

34. Please listen attentively to what I have to say. *Ātman* is within and without the orbit of the mind.

35. Even the knowers of the Vedas and *śāstras* are deluded on this point. As regards external objects, the mind gets distracted in two ways.

36-37. First, withdraw the mind from the objects of charms and temptations; second, lead it to the goal of life. When the mind is voluntarily and completely withdrawn from the charms and temptations of the world, it remains unaffected. It is important to have mastery over the dual tendency of the mind.

38. The perception of all external objects is influenced by our

conceptions of time, space, and causation. The experience of them is possible through this twofold mental operation. But consciousness itself is unlimited. Therefore, the mind's twofold operation does not apply.

39-40. Consciousness can be realized simply by withdrawing the mind from all objects. If one wants to see the image of a certain object in a mirror, he must turn his attention away from the other images and one-pointedly fix his mind on the particular image he wants to see.

41-42. If a man wants to see space in the mirror, he should remove the objects that create images in the mirror. The all-pervading void also exists in the mirror, but without removing the images, one cannot see it.

43. Space is everywhere; it is the foundation of all. Therefore, when all objects are taken away, image-free space is clearly seen in the mirror.

44. Similarly, consciousness is all-pervasive and the foundation of all. O brahmin, like space, it is ever-present in the mind.

45. Thus, for self-realization, one simply has to withdraw the mind from all objects. O brahmin, can you find a place where consciousness is not present?

46. There is no place where consciousness is not present. Therefore, this diversity is a creation of the mind and its modifications.

47. Realization of consciousness requires absolute purity and not mere concentration of mind. That is why the self is called "unknowable." It is not subject matter and therefore the mind cannot know it.

48. The impurity of the mind lies in the thinking process. If the mind is free from thoughts, it becomes pure.

49. Now it should be clear to you that purity of mind is important for realizing the self. The self can never be realized without a pure mind.

50. How can one have knowledge unless the mind is purified? If the mind is pure, why cannot one attain knowledge? All spiritual means are meant for the purification of the mind.

51. The austerities of selfless action, selfless devotion, and the practice of non-attachment are performed for the sole purpose of purifying the mind. Otherwise, they do not serve any purpose.

52. The lord of life is seen in the purified mind.'

Hearing this from King Janaka, Aṣṭāvakra inquired further,

53. 'O king, you said that if the mind is purified by the absence of thought, pure consciousness manifests itself.

54. Then it follows that sleep can bring about self-realization and one does not need to make any effort.'

55. Hearing the confusion of Aṣṭāvakra, King Janaka said, 'Now I will resolve your doubt. Please hear me attentively.

56. It is true that in deep sleep the mind is turned away from the charms and temptations of the world. But at the same time, the mind is completely veiled by *tamas*. How can one experience the Absolute in such a condition?

57-58. If a mirror is painted black, nothing can reflect in it. Similarly, when the mind is veiled by the inertia of sleep, it is not able to respond to any illumination. It is like an eclipse of the moon.

59. Otherwise, a lump of clay or a wall could experience consciousness. Therefore, only a transparent (*sattvic*) mind can realize consciousness.

60-61. This is why an infant does not experience reality. The black color painted on the mirror is reflected in the mirror, but it does not show. Similarly, the intrinsic nature of the mirror to reflect whatever is in front of it cannot be altered, because the mirror cannot lose its intrinsic nature. Yet, because of the black paint, it is not seen.

62. Likewise, in deep sleep the mind is veiled by slumber. Therefore for lack of clarity it does not shine forth.

63. The person who is awake remembers the sleeping state. In that state of mind one can recollect the experiences of the sleeping state.

64. I will explain this clearly. Listen attentively. There are two states of mind: the first is the state of illumination; the second is the state of deliberation.

65. The inner state of illumination is experienced when one contacts external objects; the state of deliberation occurs when the objects are seen.

66. The state of illumination is *nirvikalpa* because one is not aware of the objects. When he becomes aware of the objects, that state of mind is called *savikalpa*.

67-68. Experiencing something without feeling distinctions of "this" or "that" is a state of illumination. When a verbal distinction is made, such as "this is this," then that state is the lower state of *samādhi* with seed.

69-70. This drama has two aspects. In this drama, what is seen is called "direct knowledge." That which is based on logic is called "remembered knowledge." The first category of knowledge is to realize the *saṁskāras* of the past. In this way the mind has two powers.

71-73. In deep sleep, illumination without desire exists and lasts as long as one sleeps. It is termed *jaḍasamādhi* in the scriptures. In the waking state, self-illumination seems to be diminished, yet realization of that light is considered to be a state of *savikalpa samādhi*.

In deep sleep there is undifferentiated experience, but it is completely veiled by inertia. Therefore it is a stupefied state. It is full of light but sheds its light on other objects and is unable to illuminate itself. That is why the learned ones have used the simile "Deep sleep is like an oil lamp." The limitation imposed upon the self at the beginning of manifestation may be considered to be similar to deep sleep. It is also called *avyakta*, unmanifest, and *mahāśūnya*, the great void.

74-75. The state of deep sleep is the experience of nothingness. In the waking state, the state of mind remains the same as in deep sleep, although the objects are visible, but during the waking state, a new thought arises every moment. So the world of thoughts previously experienced disappears.

76. In deep sleep, the mind remains in its dormant state because there is no alternation. While seeing an object during the waking state the mind is absorbed also, but that absorption is disturbed by the experience of another object the next moment.

77. O brahmin, listen. I will explain this to you through my direct experience. Attempting to fathom the subtlety of this truth, even the learned ones become bewildered.

78. *Nirvikalpa samādhi,* the highest state of *samādhi,* deep sleep, and seeing objects directly are all three similar.

[*Note: It is the nature of the mind to assume the form of the seen, but in deep sleep, the seen remains dormant.*]

79. Those who practice and attain direct experience see the difference in those three kinds of experience. The differences are known to those who practice.

80. In *samādhi* there is only pure consciousness. In deep sleep, consciousness remains dormant. Diversity is seen in the waking state, but in *samādhi* only one absolute reality exists.

81. Throughout, self-illumined *ātman* is one and the same, and always remains free from all affliction. Therefore it is said to be pure consciousness.

82. *Samādhi* and deep sleep last for long periods, so when a person comes out of those states, he remembers them.

83. But the moment of perception is so brief that one does not have time to become familiar with this naturally arising state. If *samādhi* and deep sleep were as brief, these states would also remain unfamiliar.

84-86. In daily life, *samādhi* and sleep can be experienced for a few moments, but because of prolonged deep sleep, the wise can differentiate between sleep and *samādhi.* Those who cannot differentiate between the two cannot understand the difference. O brahmin, every human being experiences these moments, but because he is unfamiliar with *samādhi,* he does not even notice them.

87. *Samādhi* is a profound experience of desirelessness. Such a state is also experienced in sleep and sometimes in the waking state also.

88. These experienced states are not considered to be *samādhi,* because all *saṁskāras* remain latent therein, ready to manifest.

89. Instantly, one sees an object which is untainted by deliberation. This is similar to *samādhi.* Let me elaborate further. Listen reverently.

90. The unmanifest state of the self-existent reality reveals that there existed nothing, neither day nor night. It is called sleep. It is a dormant state of consciousness. Everything remained unrevealed, for there was nothing to be revealed.

91. The experience of the void is deep sleep. Here consciousness remains dormant. During the waking state one consciously recollects the experience of nothingness that was experienced during deep sleep.

92. Thus consciousness united with the knowledge of the unconscious is known as *suṣupti,* deep sleep, whereas consciousness shining in *samādhi* is identical to Brahman.

93. Consciousness experienced in *samādhi* is beyond time, space, and the awareness of nothingness. The light of lights engulfs all darkness, and pure consciousness alone exists. How can that power be the cause of deep sleep?

94. Therefore, sleep is not the ultimate goal of goals.'

Thus King Janaka removed the veil of ignorance of Aṣṭāvakra.

Thus ends Chapter 16, in which King Janaka explains the states of waking, dreaming, and sleeping.

17

The Method of *Sādhanā* Explained by King Janaka and the Analysis of Self-Realization

1. O PARAŚURĀMA, I will tell you the further questions Aṣṭāvakra posed after listening to Janaka. Listen attentively.

2-3. Aṣṭāvakra asked, 'Please explain, with full details, the varieties of momentary *samādhis.* When do those highest states of realization occur?'

The warm-hearted king responded,

4-5. 'O brahmin, listen. I will tell you about the momentary *samādhis* occurring in daily life. When a lover embraces his beloved for the first time, he is not aware of what is going on within and without, yet he is not asleep. That is a kind of awareness similar to *samādhi.*

6-7. O sage, when a *sādhaka* suddenly fulfills a burning desire, at that moment he doesn't remain aware of anything within or without, though he is not under the influence of sleep. That also is considered similar to *samādhi.*

8-9. When the mind is free from all thought-constraints and a person is walking cheerfully and unafraid, and suddenly a tiger or some other fierce animal appears, for a moment he loses his outer and inner awareness yet is fully conscious; that momentary state is also similar to *samādhi.*

10-11. When someone suddenly hears that his beloved son, who was healthy and successfully carrying on his family responsibilities, has died, for a moment that person loses his internal and external awareness and yet is fully awake. That state of sudden shock is similar to experiencing a moment of *samādhi.*

12. Listen, I will explain *samādhi* in many ways. There are moments of transition between waking, dreaming, and sleeping. Those moments are experiential and similar to *samādhi.*

13-14. Just as the leech moves from one grip to another grip, the *sādhaka* should watch the functions of the mind during those moments of transition.

15-17. You are endowed with a keen intellect. In this regard, amidst worldly activities, intelligence seems to be segmented. That intelligence differs from moment to moment, according to its activities. The pause between moments can be considered similar to *samādhi.*

18. Remember, Aṣṭāvakra, those who have profound knowledge of *samādhi* are in *samādhi* all the time. For them, every moment is *samādhi.* For the ignorant, *samādhi* does not exist any more than a rabbit's horns exist.'

19. Hearing this, Aṣṭāvakra again asked, 'O king, if in worldly activities everyone experiences moments of *samādhi,* then how does the world continue to function?

20. In deep sleep, consciousness remains unmanifest. Therefore the sleep state cannot be used to attain *samādhi.*

21. The moments of *samādhi* are experienced in the waking state, but they are not able to lead a seeker to the real state of *samādhi.* The highest state of *samādhi* is the direct experience of pure consciousness. Then how are human beings able to live in the world and conduct their worldly duties?

22. After attaining the highest state of *samādhi,* ignorance is completely dispelled. Such a state of *samādhi* liberates and bestows pure knowledge.

23. That *samādhi* occurs naturally in the instant between two

thoughts, so why are people still in bondage? O lord of Kings, please help me resolve this doubt.'

At this question, the king replied,

24. 'O brahmin, listen, I will tell you the greatest of all deep secrets. From the beginning, the world continues to function because of the darkness of ignorance.

25-26. These pleasant and painful experiences are there, and all creatures experience them, like they experience a dream. Removal of ignorance is possible only through pure knowledge.

27. To remove ignorance, one needs to have profound knowledge, which can be brought into use during the waking state. That knowledge which helps one to attain the highest state of *samādhi* will not be helpful in conducting worldly duties.

28. Just as the surface of the mirror is the foundation of all its images, self-existent knowledge stands behind and supports all that we experience.

29. That knowledge which arises from desirelessness is pure knowledge. That state in which one experiences any desire is the lower state.

30. To realize the value of ignorance with its currents and crosscurrents is also a kind of knowledge, and that is seen in cause and effect and in all forms in the world.

31-33. Not being able to realize the self-existent reality is the cause of ignorance. Self-existent reality is complete in itself because it has no limitations. It is beyond time, space, and causation. Considering the body, senses, and mind to be the self is also a function of ignorance.

34. Unless this ignorance is dispelled, worldly bondage is never broken. Without profound knowledge of *ātman,* it is impossible to break this bondage.

35-37. Knowledge is twofold: indirect and direct. Indirect knowledge is received from the scriptures and instructions given by the preceptor. But these are not means for attaining final liberation. Indirect knowledge is accepted on mere belief. It cannot bestow freedom. Direct knowledge dawns when *samādhi* is attained.

38. When *samādhi* is attained, then one also attains pure knowledge, and the same knowledge is able to liberate the aspirant.

39-41. Though ignorant people experience moments of *samādhi,* these moments are not liberating. Similarly, if one who has never seen a gem is taken to a treasury of gems, he will not recognize a gem, even though he is searching for one. But those who have seen gems can recognize them in all conditions.

42-44. Similarly, ignorant people, without knowing what *samādhi* is, are deprived of its fruits. The learned are deprived of it because the knowledge they receive comes through scripture and their preceptors. The ignorant do not know anything about the stars shining in the sky, although they can see them.

45-46. One who has heard in which quarter of the sky the planet Venus shines, has heard it described, and who has a keen desire to know about it—that brilliant seeker with a one-pointed mind can see the planet. But others cannot.

47. O brahmin, similarly, there are different states of *samādhi,* yet the ignorant, for lack of knowledge and the desire to know, are not aware of their real self, just as one who has a treasure deeply buried in his house is a beggar because he is not aware of it.

48-49. Therefore, all these main states of *samādhi* are of no value if there is no knowledge of them. Children are pure and their minds and hearts remain unpolluted with worldly desires and thoughts. Though they seem to be in a state of *samādhi,* yet such a state does not liberate them from the bondage of ignorance.

The first step of *samādhi* is called *savikalpa samādhi* and that *savikalpa samādhi* is able to destroy ignorance for the betterment of the world.

50-51. When sincere efforts to know the truth are made in many lifetimes, the pure self blesses the seeker from within and then he is inspired to attain liberation. Otherwise, for millions of years, such an opportunity does not arise.

52. To be born in the world endowed with intelligence is very difficult and to have a one-pointed, inward mind is the most difficult of all.

53-54. O brahmin, the non-sentient and sentient exist in the world, and human beings also exist. Among human beings, millions live like animals and have no knowledge of truth, untruth, sin, and virtue.

55-56. Millions of people motivated by worldly desire are engaged in the world and caught in its charms and temptations. The learned ones, proud of their learning, have a desire for heavenly joys.

57. A fortunate few who are endowed with the faculty of discrimination still do not know how to purify their minds and hearts. Therefore, they deprive themselves of the attainment of the highest state.

58. That highest state of consciousness is veiled by maya. How can those who are blinded by maya attain *mokṣa*? That is why such ignorant ones can never attain *samādhi,* the highest state.

59. There are a few unfortunate ones who, though they understand the importance of liberation, get so caught in the whirlpool of their emotions that they lose that opportunity, like one who, possessing a gem, throws it away without knowing its worth.

60. Oh, how powerful is the veil of maya, that some even have the ability to attain *samādhi* but are lost in the jungle of their thinking and lose the gem from their hands.

61. Those fortunate ones by whose devotion the self is pleased are free from the bondage of maya and gifted with

scriptural knowledge and faith. Such rare ones attain the highest state of enlightenment.

62-65. Endowed with non-attachment, a burning desire to attain *ātman,* and immense faith, the seeker seeks the refuge of an adept and by receiving knowledge of liberation attains freedom. This knowledge is direct knowledge.

66. The only One, self-existent reality, is subject to contemplation, and by right logic one should come to understanding and dispel all doubts.

67. In this way, with full determination and firm faith, one should continue contemplating on *ātman* until he has realized it. One should make full effort.

68. "I am the pure self." One who contemplates with this single desire through meditation attains the highest state and dispels the darkness of ignorance. Do not doubt it.

69. *Nirvikalpa samādhi* is attained through the deep state of meditation. Then one constantly remembers "I am That." He should maintain that awareness with every breath of his life.

70. "I am the self-existent absolute One." Such a determination will help one to receive the knowledge that destroys the very root of ignorance and its offshoots.

71. In the highest state of meditation, the mind does not reason or desire. There are various avenues of knowledge, but the highest state of knowledge is all-pervading pure consciousness.

72. By not experiencing anything other than *ātman,* all thoughts are removed. Once they are removed, the highest state of *samādhi* is attained.

73. At this disappearance of the picture, the background remains crystal-clear. Therefore, completely removing the picture causes clarity.

74. Similarly, when free from desire, the mind becomes liberated. Therefore, renunciation of the seeds of all desires leads to the attainment of self.

75-76. Those who have purified their *buddhi* can realize the self in a moment's time. O brahmin, there are three types of seekers.

77-78. The finest seekers grasp it at once and while hearing about self-realization, their contemplation becomes spontaneous. This first category of seekers does not find any difficulty.

79-80. Long ago, on a moonlit summer night, I was sitting in a green garden on a costly, well-decorated seat. My beloved was embracing me, and my eyes were drowsy with wine. During that time I heard sweet words coming down from heaven. Those words were full of praise of one absolute, without a second. The same moment, I realized the highest state.

81-83. Then and there, through my introspective power, I attained that auspicious state and remained in that blissful ocean. After being aware of the conscious state of my mind, I started thinking that state was wondrous and full of overwhelming bliss.

84. Today I have attained that state beyond. Now I maintain it. The pleasures of the senses are valueless in comparison with that blissful state.

85-86. Even the pleasures available in Brahmaloka, the heavenly kingdom of the creator, cannot be compared to this. Up until now I have been wasting my time, like a person who does not realize his coffers are filled with treasure and wanders begging.

87. Alas, people are unaware of the blissful joy of *ātman*. They make great effort to gratify their senses and do not experience the everlasting bliss that resides within.

88. I do not need to make any effort to gain worldly pleasures. I always remain in a blissful state.

89. What have I to do with external activities in life? It is like crushing and using the same spices again and again until they no longer have any flavor.

90-91. Every day I find the same dishes of food, the same kinds of garlands, the court, valuable ornaments, and damsels.

Even while enjoying these objects, I find their beauty fading. Still, people use them, as sheep follow other sheep. This is constantly going on and now I hate these objects.

92. Having made this decision, when I wanted to go into meditation, another auspicious thought dawned.

93-94. I started thinking, "Oh, what has happened to me? I am that self which is full of bliss. I am That. Then what more do I want? What else do I have to achieve? What have I not already achieved? What is unobtainable?

95. Can we ever attain that which is not attained? My essential nature is everlasting bliss. How can I be engaged in actions?

96. Body, senses, and internal organs are as unreal as dreams. I am the indivisible consciousness. All things belong to me.

97-99. What great experience can be attained just by controlling one of these inner instruments. This way, if I control one mind, what good is that? Now I am aware that I have many controlled and uncontrolled minds in me. If I have perfect control of all minds and not my own mind, how will it help me? I am limitless sky. How is it possible for me to control the limitless?

100-101. In this way, I am complete unto myself. Why do I need *samādhi*? I am full of bliss and more omniscient than the sky. Then how can I do good or bad actions?

102. Innumerable bodies and souls live by my grace. How am I concerned with any action, and what have I to do with it? Therefore, I have no duty. Neither am I doer nor non-doer.

103. I am full of bliss. What will I gain from the control of my internal states? Whether I am in *samādhi* or not, I am the truth and am omnipresent.

104-5. The state in which my body is, let it be in that state. I remain in full bliss unto myself. I am fully illumined, perfect, and pure."

106-7. The third category of seeker receives the fruits of his austerities in several lifetimes. The second category of aspirant attains knowledge systematically, listening to the great adepts. Contemplating on that knowledge, they attain the state beyond.

108. Why attain *nirvikalpa samādhi* without having its wisdom? Even if a seeker experiences it hundreds of times, it will not liberate him. Therefore, momentary *samādhi* attained during the waking state is in vain.

109. Absolute knowledge is pure in its nature, and this is our essential nature. Knowing this fact, under the influence of thoughts and desires, one does not realize it. If all thoughts, imagination, and emotions are completely shunned, that which is self-illumined would be ever-green, ever-young, ever-free.

110. The knowledge that is experienced during *nirvikalpa samādhi* is pure knowledge. It is ever-present, unalloyed, and free from blemish. How can it be experienced?

111-12. Pure consciousness is the background on which the phenomenal world is seen. Therefore, it must manifest itself with all its purity. It remains unnoticed because it is not distinguished from the phenomena which are displayed by it. If you remove all of these phenomena, it shines like a clear crystal. This is the shortest method of self-realization.

113. O brahmin, contemplate on what you have learned and you will realize the self. Then you will receive wisdom, which will bestow eternal happiness on you.'

114-15. Thus Aṣṭāvakra received instructions from the wise king. Janaka paid due homage and bid him farewell. Aṣṭāvakra returned home and attained direct self-realization by discriminating, contemplating, and meditating. All his doubt vanished. He became a *jīvanmukta,* liberated in the same lifetime."

Thus ends Chapter 17, the dialogue in which King Janaka imparts the knowledge of different aspects of samādhi to Sage Aṣṭāvakra and finally leads him to the highest state of samādhi.

18

Dattātreya Elaborates on the Dialogue on Knowledge Between King Janaka and Aṣṭāvakra

1. DATTĀTREYA SAID, "Paraśurāma, I explained the nature of pure consciousness which cannot ordinarily be known, and also I explained the state of *samādhi,* which one experiences on different occasions in daily life.

2. But people, deluded by maya, do not notice these moments. Knowledge of the absolute is possible only through an inward and one-pointed mind. There is no other means.

3. Paraśurāma, what good is this lengthy discussion? I will give you the essence. Through the mind, you can see the objects of the world, but the mind is an object itself.

4. Mind continues to exist even when there are no objects for it to contact. Pure mind without an object is pure knowledge.

5. Pure knowledge is eternally illumined. In obtaining such knowledge, we cannot depend on any other object because those objects will also be dependent on other objects. Then, in the absence of the self-illumined cause, there will be darkness everywhere.

6. O son of Bhṛgu, do you not experience yourself at the same time that you experience other objects? If you do not, then you yourself do not exist! Then how will you question, and whom?

7. If you do not exist any more than a flower in the sky, then why do you want to know yourself? How can I prove the existence of your self to you?

8. You have general knowledge regarding your existence, but you do not know yourself in reality. Your essential nature is indestructible.

9. One whose doubts are completely removed realizes his true self. I wonder, having known the self, why are you deluded?

10. That knowledge which illuminates all is pure knowledge. You cannot be excluded because you, yourself, are illumined.

11-12. You identify yourself with the body because body-consciousness makes you think that way. Think subtly. When you experience something other than your body, do you also experience your body at the same time? In that case, everything related to you could be considered to be your body.

13. Whatever you determine to be, and identify yourself with, that you are. In this way, you will become one with everything. Then how can you be body alone?

14. But you cannot be the objects of your experience, because all these objects are continually changing. Therefore your true nature is knowledge, not the transient objects of knowledge.

15. That knowledge, identical with the self, is ever-illumined. It is never contaminated by the particular objects which it illumines. That radiant knowledge is stamped with the diverse impressions of the body, time, place, and so on.

16-17. That which remains, after removing all thoughts and desires, is consciousness, or *ātman,* your true self. Ignorance, the root cause of birth and death, vanishes forever after one catches a glimpse of that self-existent reality.

18. Liberation is found neither above the sky, nor below it, nor on the surface of the earth. Renunciation of *saṅkalpa* is the cause of liberation.

19. *Mokṣa* is self-realization. That is why it is ever-present. Only through non-attachment can one attain liberation.

20. There is no other way of attaining liberation. To become the doer is self-destruction. If you identify yourself with your body, it will be like imagining horns on a rabbit.

21. The self is perfect in all aspects, so there can be no liberation anywhere else. If liberation is synonymous with the self, then like a mirror and its reflection, it is identical with the self.

22. Even ordinary people know that liberation is their essential nature. It is freedom from the bondage of ignorance.

23-27. To accept the nature of any object as both real and unreal is self-contradictory. Someone may declare that objects obtained in a dream are real and those obtained in the waking state are unreal. Listen further. That which does not exist permanently is unreal. The objects of the world are not everlasting. Therefore they are unreal. That which causes bondage is not real.

28. To be constantly established in consciousness is *mokṣa.* Renouncing the objects, consciousness alone exists.

29. To be aware of the objects is to limit consciousness. When one is not aware of the objects, then consciousness is seen in its perfection.

30. If someone says that consciousness is experienced only within the confines of time and space, then tell me whether time and space themselves are not also illumined by consciousness.

31-32. That which is not illumined by the self-existent reality can never exist. If it exists, it will be self-existent reality. All the objects of the world are limited by time, but time and all the objects of the universe are within pure consciousness. That is why you can visualize them.

33. How will you know those objects which you consider to be unillumined? Because consciousness is all-pervading and unqualified, it can be differentiated only if there is another self-illumined consciousness.

34. The existence of any object cannot be proven without consciousness, because an object separate from consciousness does not exist.

35. The center of consciousness and consciousness are virtually one and the same. They cannot be separated any more than a ray of light can be separated from its source. If they are separated, there will be no way of proving their existence.

36. Therefore all external objects, even those which are not comprehended, are pervaded by consciousness. Thus, all illumined objects should be realized in the ovum of consciousness.

37-38. How can that which is one absolute be divided into pieces? O Paraśurāma, think wisely. That object which seems to exist in consciousness is only a reflection, exactly like the reflection of the sun seen in a mirror. One object that is covered by another is not seen.

39. O Paraśurāma, if we admit this, then there will be serious confusion. We have already discussed this. External objects create confusion.

40-42. Then how can we prove the transitory nature of any object? Therefore the self-illumined *ātman,* with its own power of consciousness, exists everywhere. Nothing exists except one."

Hearing the sermon of Dattātreya, the sage Paraśurāma inquired, "O lord, whatever you have explained seems impossible. One absolute consciousness seen as many is impossible.

43. Everyone thinks that consciousness and objects are two different elements, but objects are never found outside consciousness. Therefore I agree that objects are seen with the help of consciousness and I also agree that consciousness is self-illumined.

44-45. Just as the seer is different from the seen, likewise consciousness seems to be different from its source. But consciousness and its source are one and the same. I cannot assimilate this knowledge. How can the law and the lawgiver be one and the same?

46-47. King Janaka said that if the mind is free from all conflicting thoughts, then mind attains one-pointedness. This is the prime means of attaining the highest knowledge. That is the real nature of *ātman.*

48. If *ātman* did not have the mind as its instrument, then how could there be differentiation between animate and inanimate objects?

49. The mind is the cause of both bondage and liberation. The mind, filled with desire, causes bondage. Free from all desires, the mind becomes the means of liberation.

50. How can the mind become *ātman* when the mind is only an instrument? Mind without desire is the means for liberation, yet there seems to be duality in your philosophy.

51. Usually, in daily life, when the mind becomes deluded, it is not considered to be truth. Delusion itself is not untrue. In such a case, how can there be absence of duality?

52. That which is non-existent cannot function, but all the objects of the world seem to exist and, through them, the work of the world continues.

53. So tell me, how can they be unreal? How can that be unreal which is the means of attaining the absolute? If all cognition creates delusion, how can one distinguish what is delusion from what is not?

54. Please also tell me, *gurudeva,* why is everyone going through this delusion? I am terribly perplexed."

55. Dattātreya, the knower of truth, was pleased with such a good question and began explaining,

56. "Paraśurāma, you have asked a wonderful question. We have already discussed this, but as long as one is not fully satisfied, one should continue contemplating.

57. If the disciple does not express his doubts in front of his *gurudeva,* how can these doubts be removed? All individuals have different types of intellects, and there are different methods of removing their doubts.

58-59. Therefore, without asking questions in his own

specific manner and with specific purpose, how can one overcome his doubts? Putting questions in front of the *gurudeva* is the proper way of receiving knowledge from him.

60. The one absolute reality seems to be seen in many ways. This is possible in the way a mirror is one but, because of numerous images, is seen in many ways.

61. In the dream state the mind is the creator, the seer, and the seen. Similarly, pure consciousness alone assumes all forms: the seer, the process of seeing, and the object seen.

62-63. Even without light, a blind man can sense an object. Although he does not see its form, he experiences it through touch. But in the absence of consciousness, nobody is able to experience anything.

64-65. Without a mirror, no reflection can be seen. That is why it seems as though mirror and reflection are one and the same. Similarly, without consciousness, the mind cannot exist.

66. Just as in a dream, dream objects and the mind become one, similarly, the mind does not have a separate existence in the waking state. Exactly like in a dream, in the waking state the mind seems to function in the world. This is shared imagination.

67. In the dreaming state, cutting a tree with an axe is imaginary. O Paraśurāma, if the activity in the dream is not true, how can the means of that dream be true?

68. Human beings do not have horns. Therefore, to believe that one is being injured by the horns of a human is false. Get rid of false imagination. O Paraśurāma, in the dreaming state, the mind is the cause of false projections.

69. During the dreaming state, the cause of the dream and the dream itself is the mind; similarly, in the waking state, the mind does not exist apart from the objects it experiences.

70-71. Pure consciousness through its sovereignty sometimes expresses itself as the seer and other times as the seen. At times it remains in a state of *samādhi.*

72. O son of Bhṛgu, listen. Pure consciousness is all-pervading in itself. Therefore it cannot be compared with the void, because it is self-illumined. Apart from this, there is no difference.

73-74. Like the void, the self is perfect, subtle, pure, unborn, infinite, formless, the source of all, uncontaminated, immanent, and transcendent. The void does not have these qualities. In reality, pure consciousness is called the real self. Among all this, the self alone exists. The pure self is called *ātman.*

75. Because consciousness pervades all, there is no difference between the self and the void. That which is the void is called *ātman* and that which is *ātman* is called the void.

76. Out of delusion, the ignorant conceive of *ātman* in the form of space in the same way an owl perceives sunlight in the form of darkness.

77-79. The wise man sees the void as that self-illumined consciousness. The supreme power exists beyond the phenomenal world, yet manifests itself in many forms. Through her power, O Paraśurāma, she assumes different forms.

80. She appears in many ways, but this is because of the distortion of the mind. Actually she is pure consciousness, self-existent reality.

81. As the magician by his skill creates many forms, yet remains all alone, similarly, pure consciousness is free from all impurities.

82-83. By the veil of maya, she seems to be many, though she is only one pure consciousness beyond all comprehension. Her veiling power confuses those who have limited knowledge, just like a magician confuses his audience.

84. Maya is unknowable. We see that yogis and others with the power of mantra perform miracles with their limited powers, but nothing is impossible for the highest consciousness.

85. In the world, we see that magicians with their skills

perform many wonders. Therefore, it is not difficult for absolute consciousness.

86-87. O Paraśurāma, supreme consciousness, through her pure power of sovereignty, allows herself to appear in many forms. Egotism is the cause of separateness and is the same as limited *buddhi,* which is called *avidyā.*

88. By not contemplating on the real self and by being dissipated in the external world, many logicians and learned pandits get deluded.

89-90. Unless someone makes practical application of his guru's teachings about reality and unreality and employs them for self-realization, merely listening to instructions cannot bring the fruit of liberation. Therefore, Paraśurāma, experience everything I have taught you so far through your inward and one-pointed mind.

91. Remove the different forms of the world and be aware of the underlying unity in diversity. That supreme power is self-illumined because it is free from illusions.

92. Therefore, she is the creator of the pause, and the pause itself is yet beyond all. All insentient objects rest in her and their existence depends on the self-existent *ātman.*

93-94. These objects have no power to illumine themselves. Therefore they are not self-existent. The self-existent consciousness does not depend on any external power for illumination. It is the highest of all and is not found in insentient objects.

95. Therefore, self-conscious reality is free from diversities and remains untouched by limitation. It is not like the images in the mirror.

96-97. O Paraśurāma, such an all-pervading consciousness cannot be divided, because it is self-existent reality. The same consciousness is called all-pervading, one, absolute reality.

98-99. For the sake of discussion this self-existent reality seems to have a dual existence, although it is actually one all-pervading reality. As light and warmth are inseparable from fire, similarly the absolute reality is inseparable from blissful joy.

100-101. This is also called *māyā śakti,* which can make the impossible possible. It is like a mirror that is crystal-clear, yet contains images.

102. The appearance of limitation is the appearance of the non-self. This is called *avidyā* (ignorance), *jaḍaśakti* (unconscious power), *śūnya* (void), and *prakṛti* (the primordial nature).

103-4. The first stage of limitation is called non-existence, void, austerity, darkness, or the beginning of creation. The appearance of the void is due to ignorance.

105. The sphere of *ātman* is free from egotism, and that state is called the void. Egotism is the cause of *samsara,* the world.

106-8. That which the ignorant think is the void actually gives birth to the various forms of the world. O Paraśurāma, think with clarity of mind. That which you consider the void is actually the ovum of all living creatures. The void, seen in the body of others, is actually the self-existent *ātman.*

109-10. The veil of ignorance has its predominance and that is considered to be the mind. The center of consciousness is called the individual soul.

111-14. Thus, the same *ātman,* the universal self, or consciousness, appears as the void and then becomes the five elements: earth, water, fire, air, and space. Space or void is very subtle and clear, but because of the qualities of *tamas,* the five elements are seen in it. In this way, covered by the body, it becomes the individual soul and illumines within, like a candle kept in a jar illumines the jar. As the light is seen through the holes of the jar, similarly, the light of *ātman* emanates through the senses.

115-16. Consciousness, though all-pervading, is not involved at all in creation, but when its conscious power removes its veil, then one can see it. Because of the light of consciousness, the darkness of the mind is removed.

117. Therefore, O Paraśurāma, mind has no separate existence. For practical purposes, the individual soul assumes the

form of the mind. Consciousness which seems to move is called "mind," and that which does not move is called "self."

118. O Paraśurāma, removing the veil of ignorance is the nature of consciousness; this veil is called *vikalpa* and when that *vikalpa* does not exist, that knowledge is liberation.

119-20. O Paraśurāma, renounce this doubt that by removing *saṅkalpa* and *vikalpa,* ignorance can again influence your individual being, because actually, there is no veil. The veil is self-imagined.

121-22. Suppose someone imagines that he has been harassed and tortured by his enemy, and he is constantly nagged. But when he renounces that imagination, his fear also disappears. Then where is the bondage?

123-124. O Paraśurāma, from the very beginning there is no bondage. This insentient delusion should be removed, and then you will know what bondage is. To believe that one is in bondage is the greatest of all bondages. It is like a child's self-imagined fear.

125. If the wise person does not renounce this negative imagination, he cannot liberate himself from the bondage of the world and attain *mokṣa.*

126. What is this bondage? How can it bind pure consciousness? If the images that are seen in the mirror are able to create bondage, then the appearance of fire in the mirror can also burn.

127-28. To accept that there is bondage and to believe in bondage is the cause of bondage. There is no bondage otherwise.

129-30. Unless the Mother Divine, supreme consciousness, Tripurā, Brahmā, Viṣṇu, and Śaṅkara bless the seeker so that he purifies his inner being, nobody can help a seeker attain liberation. In this way, O Paraśurāma, renounce this false sense of bondage and self-created existence of the mind and be happy.

131. Though the mind exists in *nirvikalpa samādhi,* that existence is actually *ātman* and there is no duality in it.

132. Apart from the awareness of "this" and "that," there is

no mind. The moment the concept of "this and that" is removed, the self alone exists.

133. The confusion of seeing a snake in a rope happens only on the basis of the object (the rope), which is considered to be real. Therefore, consciousness illumines the snake in a rope.

134. Removal or abandonment *(bādha)* of the snake in the rope is due to acknowledging the rope as such. When you see the rope as a snake, that is not knowledge.

135. But in the example of the dream in which we see a rope, the rope itself exists in consciousness. When the dream is over, the rope disappears, and yet consciousness remains.

136. Thus, not the objects of waking or dreaming, but consciousness alone is the self-existent reality. Then where does duality exist?

137. If you think that external objects are real because they seem to be real and because worldly purposes are accomplished through them, listen. Even the objects of dreams seem to be real during the dreaming state.

138-39. There is one difference between the experience of the waking and dreaming states. In the waking state one knows the falsehood of the dreaming state, but in the dreaming state one does not realize the falsehood of the waking state. With this weak argument, it cannot be concluded that the experiences of the waking state are true.

140. Are not the objects of a dream useful during the dream, just as material objects are useful during wakefulness? As we experience the steadiness of the objects in the waking state, do we not experience the objects in the dreaming state in exactly the same way?

141. The objects seen in dreams are not real in the waking state, and the objects seen in the waking state are not real in the dream state. This similarity is found in both states.

142-43. If you think attentively, what is the difference between the past events of the waking state and the events of the dreaming state? If the magician creates objects through his illusory power, do you think that his creation is true?

144. The difference between true and untrue is not known to ordinary people, and because of the attachment to the objects of the world, they say that the objects of the world are true.

145. O Paraśurāma, the truth is self-evident and ever-existent. Worldly objects, on the other hand, are transitory and evident only when perceived.

146. The worldly objects are seen differently at different times. But, O Paraśurāma, contemplate how and where consciousness is absent.

147. When one is aware of *ātman,* or consciousness, then how will he be aware of time? If one is not aware, then how will he be aware of consciousness and time both? Because the awareness in both cases is due to the illumination of pure consciousness.

148. Therefore, O Paraśurāma, consciousness is all-pervading illumination. That is why it is truth. What is truth and what is untruth? Let me briefly explain.

149. That which does not depend on anything for its illumination is truth. In other cases, it is untrue, exactly like the snake in the rope is untrue.

150. Contradictory statements can prove the validity of self-existent reality. Contradiction itself is proof of invalidity. Verbal denial is mental admittance, in a way. Contradiction leads nowhere and does not furnish any proof.

151. Therefore that which is self-evident, unconditioned, and the very foundation of all experience is real. Anything other than this is unreal.

152-53. Unless there is self-conscious, self-existent reality, nothing can be experienced. Even the notion "it is nothing" cannot be experienced without consciousness. Therefore a logician who claims that consciousness is not the source of illumination is like a man who does not admit his own existence. If he tries to prove that he does not exist, what is the source of the denial? How can a person who, because of lack of self-realization, doubts his own existence still claim to remove the ignorance of others?

154. Even though his logic may be sound and his words flowery, he cannot lead others toward self-realization, because his knowledge is based on logic.

155-57. The knowledge which we use in our daily life is unable to prove its validity. Doubtless this so-called knowledge is deluding. Therefore it should be considered to be only an illusion. As any illusion, unless clarified, is taken as truth, similarly, in the waking state all experiences seem to be valid.

158-59. When one has profound knowledge of mother-of-pearl, he does not get deluded by mistaking it for a piece of silver. Similarly, the knowledge of the *ātman* dispels all other illusions. As everyone thinks the sky is blue though it is not, similarly, because of ignorance, the experience of the waking state is illusory. Complete freedom from illusion is pure knowledge and that is the real existence of *ātman*.

160. O Paraśurāma, I have replied to your questions decisively. Remove your doubt in this regard, decide firmly and follow it.

161. You have previously asked me how liberation is attained. Now here is the answer. Listen to me attentively.

162. In the world, there are three kinds of great liberated beings: first, second, and third. Those who constantly remain disgusted with the things of the world every moment, yet are self-realized, are the third category.

163. The second category are those who reap the fruits of actions performed in previous lives and remain in a state of *samādhi*.

164. Those who have reaped the fruits of their actions from previous lives, and were never trapped by the charms of the world, remain undisturbed in all circumstances.

165. Their temper remains even in all events of life.

166. From within, their state of mind remains tranquil. They are the best of all.

167. In this way, having different faculties of discrimination, the liberated ones are of different types, and their behavior differs according to their inner nature."

Thus ends Chapter 18, with the dialogue on gaining knowledge between King Janaka and Aṣṭāvakra.

19

The Dialogue Between the Great Seer Dattātreya and the Sage Paraśurāma on the Various States of the Realized Ones

1. HEARING FROM SAGE DATTĀTREYA, Śrī Paraśurāma started asking questions regarding the liberated ones and their behavior.

2. "Lord, kindly explain to me systematically, with full details, why differences are seen among the liberated ones.

3. It is true that all liberated ones have knowledge of the self equally and because of that knowledge, the goal of all is liberation.

4. How can there be differences if the faculty of discrimination differs? Are there different ways of realizing the self? Please tell me everything."

5-6. The compassionate Dattātreya then started explaining thoroughly, "Listen, Paraśurāma. I am revealing the highest secret to you; the means for attaining knowledge are not different nor multifarious.

7-8. One reaps the fruits according to the way he does *sādhanā.* The end of *sādhanā* is the attainment of knowledge. When *sādhanā* is not completed, more effort is needed.

9. Consciousness is knowledge and is self-illumined. For that self-existent illumination, no *sādhanā* is necessary.

10. The self-illumined *ātman* is preserved within and is crystal-clear by nature. What *sādhanā* is needed for that which is self-illumined and self-exisent?

11-13. It is preserved within *citta*, like a brilliant gem that is veiled by a deep layer of dirt and hence remains unseen. One can see it with a one-pointed mind. Then alone can one realize its full brilliance. *Sādhanā* dispels all the desires which create barriers.

14-15. In some it is noticed that desires have diminished and it is noticed that *buddhi* (the faculty of discrimination) is sharpened. There are many categories of intellect. O Paraśurāma, the degree of effort the *sādhaka* needs to make is according to the degree of ignorance which has veiled consciousness.

16. There are three main, injurious, impure desires: *aparādha vāsanā, karma vāsanā,* and *kāma vāsanā.*

17. Not having faith in the Vedas and scriptures is called *aparādha vāsanā,* and to have doubt in the existence of the self is also *aparādha vāsanā.*

18. Often those who are skilled in different arts and have the opportunity to be in the company of a sage and to study the scriptures still do not attain that knowledge beyond.

19-20. They believe that no such thing as higher knowledge exists, and even if it does exist, nobody can attain it. If one has known it, he starts doubting it. So how can doubtful knowledge become the means for liberation? In this way self-conflicting doubts create delusion.

21. This first kind of *vāsanā* is called self-created illusion. Suffering from such ignorance, hundreds of thousands of people are caught in this whirlpool.

22-23. Impurity of intellect caused by previous *saṁskāras* is called *karma vāsanā.* It creates barriers in understanding the teachings imparted by the master. These strong barriers cannot be removed by merely controlling the mind and its modifications.

24. The third one, impure desire or *kāma vāsanā,* is even

more injurious, and it is *kartavyaśeṣa,* the false sense that "this is my duty." This has many ramifications.

25-26. "This is my duty." The desire to fulfill one's duty is called *kāma vāsanā.* O Paraśurāma, someone might count the waves of the ocean, others count the atoms of the universe, and yet others count the stars, but it is impossible to count the countless desires of the human being. This third category of impurity is the desire to enjoy.

27. O Paraśurāma, this desire is filled with expectation. It is vaster than the sky and as immovable as the mountains.

28-29. Because of this selfish desire, the whole world seems to be crazy. The whole world goes through pain as if it has been burned by fire. Those fortunate ones who have attained perfect *vairāgya* (non-attachment) are liberated while living in the world. They remain calm and tranquil.

30. The mind is afflicted by these three kinds of desires. That is why supreme consciousness does not shine forth.

31. The purpose of *sādhanā* is to destroy all pleasure-seeking desires. The first category of desire is caused by lack of firm faith.

32. Freedom from the bondage of karma can be obtained by the grace of God. It is attained in many lifetimes, and not through the thousands of means one applies.

33. *Kāma vāsanā,* the desire for self-indulgence, can be removed with the help of non-attachment. Non-attachment grows when one becomes indifferent to the objects of enjoyment. There is no other way.

34. O Paraśurāma, these self-inflicted desires have a dual nature—momentary and lasting. According to their strength, efforts are made to gain release.

35-36. The root cause of various methods of *sādhanā* is the desire for liberation. Without sincere desire for liberation, no matter how much a person listens to a teacher or contemplates, he cannot attain the knowledge of self-existent reality. Sermons and accomplishments are mere skills. Mastery in any skill does not lead to the highest goal.

37. Without burning desire for liberation, study and contemplation are useless, like dressing a corpse.

38. O Paraśurāma, if the desire for liberation is weak, then that desire is in vain, just as by hearing the name of the fruit, the fruit is not obtained.

39. After receiving the fruits of an action, the desire for the fruit vanishes. Who is that human who does not have the desire to receive the fruits of his action?

40. Momentary desire for liberation, which for some reason arises all of a sudden, does not yield fruits. Intense and continuous one-pointed desire for liberation will be fruitful.

41. That intense desire for liberation inspires one on the path of *sādhanā.* This is called a burning desire.

42-43. When all limbs of a man's body are burning with a skin disease, that man desires relief. Similarly, when there is no other desire except the desire for liberation, then that yields the fruits of *mokṣa.* A desire other than for *mokṣa* is common.

44. With the help of pure non-attachment, the desire for liberation strengthens. When one becomes indifferent to the objects of enjoyment, the desire for liberation increases.

45-46. Through non-attachment comes desire for liberation, and thus one is inspired to do intense practice. From this comes increased absorption into intensive practice. The more a person is absorbed in practice, the sooner he attains the result."

47-48. Hearing the words of Dattātreya, Paraśurāma, with the desire of clarifying his confusion, asked, "O master, first you said that *satsaṅga,* the company of the sages, is the main means of liberation. Then you said it is the grace of God, and again you say by seeing the imperfections in the objects of the world, one strengthens non-attachment. Which is the prime means of attaining *mokṣa* and how can that means be attained? It is definite that nothing happens without a reason.

49. Therefore, how can intense desire, the means of liberation, be causeless? Please kindly explain in detail."

50. Compassionate Dattātreya spoke, "O Paraśurāma, listen to the foremost path leading to the final goal.

51-52. Pure consciousness, through her power of will, projected the image of the universe within herself like the images in a mirror. That power assumed the form of Hiraṇyagarbha, the firstborn, with the desire to dispel the darkness of ignorance from human beings, and created scriptures, like an ocean of knowledge.

53-54. In the world, individuals have many types of desires. With the thought of benefiting them, Hiraṇyagarbha created wish-yielding objects of the world.

55-56. Human beings by nature perform good and evil karmas. To accomplish a particular purpose in life, they are born as human beings and then become the slaves of their own karmas as they continue performing karmas.

57. "No obstacle arises in fulfilling my desire." With such an exclusive desire, one surrenders himself to God. He studies the scriptures to understand God.

58-59. Listening to the results of the *sādhanā* and motivated by its fruits, he begins to practice, but in the midst of practicing, he commits a mistake and does not obtain the desired fruit. Then he seeks the company of an adept.

60-61. Benefited by the company of the wise and listening to them regarding the highest reality, by the grace of the great Lord he starts treading the path with full vigor. In the company of the sages his good past deeds help him in climbing the ladder of *sādhanā* systematically.

62-64. In this way *satsaṅga*, company of the saints, is the prime cause for attaining the highest good. However, sometimes with the fruition of great virtuous deeds or rigorous austerities, the highest good is attained suddenly like a fruit bestowed from the sky. The state of attainment of *sādhakas* varies.

65. One whose mind is free from the impurities of the desire for enjoyment attains knowledge with little effort.

66. One whose mind has no tinge of selfish desire attains knowledge in a short time.

67. One whose mind is enveloped by desires attains only a glimpse of knowledge.

68. Such a seeker makes efforts for a long time to attain pure knowledge. That is the reason the seekers differ in their behavior.

69. O Paraśurāma, these differences indicate differing degrees of ignorance. That is why the seekers appear different.

70-71. O Paraśurāma, observe the different states of the seekers. Brahmā, Viṣṇu, and Mahādeva—these three are self-enlightened by nature. But they are different according to their nature and qualities.

72. We cannot say that they are not fully enlightened, but their nature and qualities are different.

73. As a fair-complexioned *jñānī* does not become dark, similarly, the nature of the mind does not change.

74. O Paraśurāma, look at me and my brothers. We are three illumined sons of Atri, but Durvāsā, Candramā, and myself have vast differences in our states of mind.

75. Durvāsā is easily agitated. Candramā is an enjoyer of objects, and I have renounced all identification. Look at Vasiṣṭha, who continually performs ceremonies, while Sanaka and others are renunciates.

76. Nārada is absorbed in devotion. The son of Bhṛgu, Śukrācārya, supports demons and composes poetry, while Bṛhaspati grants favors to the gods.

77. Vyāsa is highly skilled and remains absorbed in writing scriptures. See Janaka. He lives as a king, while Bharata renounced his kingdom.

78. O Paraśurāma, similarly, you can see many other yogis with different characteristics. I will tell you the reason behind it. Listen to me.

79. I have explained the three types of impurities of the mind. Among them the second one, karmic impurity, is the worst.

80. Those whose minds are not tainted with this impurity are *medhāvins,* quick to grasp and able to retain. The environment of their present life does not bind them.

81-83. For them, neither the practice of meditation nor non-attachment is necessary, nor does *samādhi* become a prerequisite for liberation. By being free from all desires, no doubt they attain the highest state of knowledge and become examples like Janaka, who was a liberated being.

84. Their faculty of discrimination is very one-pointed and pure. Therefore, they do not need to control their desires.

85-86. Even knowing the absolute, impressions of old *saṁskāras* continue to exist. Such a pure mind does not identify itself with ignorance. Learned people call them liberated and great men.

87-88. O Paraśurāma, one whose mind becomes dense as a result of attaining the fruits of his actions will not attain knowledge, even if Śaṅkara becomes his teacher. Similarly, the practitioner whose mind is not free of skepticism does not attain knowledge.

89-91. Those who are less skeptical and have minimum desires attain knowledge only after studying, contemplating, meditating, and making efforts for a long time.

92. In certain cases, the seekers are not firmly established in their practice. Therefore, in them a few desires still exist because their minds are not completely purified.

93. They are called even-minded and their state of mind is comparatively lower than that of the higher *sādhakas.* They are only practitioners, but the first and second categories of adepts are liberated.

94. All the knowers of truth have to reap the fruits of their actions. Therefore they remain under the influence of their past karmas and are free and liberated only after death.

95-96. However, the higher order of *sādhakas,* with their purified minds, have overcome such karmas. These adepts have no desires, so the karmas do not sprout.

97-98. Just as a highly skilled person can efficiently perform several actions simultaneously without making a mistake, there are some *jñānīs* who can do many things at the same time effortlessly.

99-100. A human being walks, speaks, and works with his hands at the same time. How can he do three different things, having only one mind? A teacher can easily detect those students who mispronounce during recitations, even though the class is large.

101. O Paraśurāma, you killed the great warrior, King Sahasrārjuna, who was highly skilled and used many weapons at once, yet his weapons never missed their target. You have seen it.

102-3. The minds of these accomplished ones perform many actions simultaneously. Similarly, the inner being of the highest order of adepts remains undisturbed while the adepts are working in the world. They are a special category of people.

104-5 The moment karma sprouts in their minds, it is burned by the fire of knowledge. Old *saṁskāras* are like the sprouts of the seed of desire. This is the cause of pain and pleasure. But when the sprout is burned, how can it yield fruits?

106-7. When old people play with children and the toy breaks, they express the same grief and sorrow as the children do. Similarly, adepts express pleasure and pain in the midst of their actions.

108. As a person whose mind is concentrated somewhere else experiences his grief or pleasure superficially, but never from within, likewise, while acting in the world, the internal being of an adept remains undisturbed in all conditions.

109-12. These highest adepts neither have to work toward replacing their negative desires with positive ones, nor have to restrain any sort of mental modifications. Among this higher category of adepts, some are seen occupied with work and some enjoying the objects of the world, and others losing their temper, and so on.

As we have discussed, the lower category of seeker already has a firm conviction about what is true and what is untrue. But while realizing the self or attaining *samādhi,* he remains unaffected by the subtle impressions of his past karmas. However, in other states, he can be affected by the impulses of joy or grief.

113-14. Actually, realizing the self is called *samādhi.* There is nothing beyond that. One, absolute, self-existent *ātman* is the very foundation of all activities.

115. If it doesn't exist, nothing will happen. From different internal states of knowledge arises *nirvikalpa samādhi,* the highest state of *samādhi.*

116-17. From the viewpoint of realized adepts, consciousness is entirely different from the external world, even while they seem to be active in the world. Those who have understood the unreality of the blueness of the sky still see the sky as blue though they are fully aware of the unreality of the color.

Likewise, though they are pragmatic in daily life, adepts are fully aware that reality is like the void. Had it not been like that, there would be no difference between the seer and the seen.

118-19. After knowing the unreality of external objects, an adept is not influenced by them even while experiencing them. That is why for the highest of adepts, pure consciousness is not an object. The adepts who are constantly aware of *ātman* remain in a state of no-mind. For them, the experience of the external world has ceased.

120. When the mind is centered in the self, it is called the state of *unmanī,* the transcendental mind, and when it becomes associated with external objects, considering them to be real, that is called an unsteady mind.

121. The highest adepts are like the citizens of two states. O Paraśurāma, such an adept lives in the world, yet simultaneously remains above.

122. Thus, in the view of adepts, consciousness is always like the void. Now I have answered all your questions."

Thus ends Chapter 19, with the explanation of the various states of realized sages.

20

The Appearance of Śrī Tripurā Sundarī and Her Teaching

1-6. DATTĀTREYA SAID, "Let me tell you an ancient story. Listen. Once upon a time in Satyaloka (the highest celestial realm), the sages were engaged in an earnest conversation about knowledge. Participants discussed the subtlest philosophies. The sages present included Sanaka, Vasiṣṭha, Pulastya, Pulaha, Kratu, Bhṛgu, Atri, Angirā, Pracetas, Nārada, Cyavana, Vāmadeva, Viśvāmitra, Gautama, Śukra, Parāśara, Vyāsa, Kaṇva, Kaśyapa, Dakṣa, Sumantu, Śaṅkha, Likhita, Devala, and many others. During that debate they discussed the secrets of the knowledge beyond. Then those great sages asked Brahmā, the creator,

7. 'Lord, we are all considered *jñānīs*. We are knowers of the absolute and provisional truths. Yet our states of attainment are different.

8-9. Some of us are blissful in *samādhi* all the time; some of us are engaged in contemplation; some of us are absorbed in devotion; and others are performing skillful actions.

10. Some of us are busy conducting our duties. Please let us know which is the highest category.'

11. Questioned like this, Brahmā thought, 'These sages do not have firm faith in me.' Thus he said, 'O seers, I myself do not

know this. The Lord Maheśvara is all-knowing. He must know the answer.

12-13. Let us go to him.' Thus accompanied by all the sages, Brahmā went to the abode of Śiva. Viṣṇu was also there. After greeting him, Brahmā asked the sages' question.

14-15. Hearing this, Śiva understood Brahmā's question and realized that all the sages were not endowed with firm faith and everything he said would not be acceptable. They would think according to their understanding.

16. Thinking like this, Mahādeva said, 'O sages, I am not sure about the answer. Let us meditate all together on the supreme Goddess, the source of knowledge. By her grace we can know the deepest secret.'

17-19. Hearing this from Mahādeva, Brahmā, Viṣṇu, and Mahādeva himself, with all the sages present in the assembly, started meditating on Tripurā, with the result that self-illumined Tripurā, who is the purest and the mother of speech, appeared.

20. There was a sound like a thunderbolt above. 'O seers, tell us for what purpose you have meditated on me. Express your desire. I never let my devotees' desires go unfulfilled.'

21. After listening to *parā vāk,* the unstruck sound, the sages prostrated in front of her. Brahmā and all the others started singing her praise in reverence.

22. The sages prayed to Tripurā, the goddess of knowledge itself, reverently, 'O Mother Divine, the highest of all, Śrīvidyā, with folded hands we bow in front of you.

23. You are the cause, sustenance, and annihilation of this universe. O supreme Goddess, we prostrate in front of you.

24. You are most ancient. You were never born, therefore you are ever-fresh because you never go to decay.

25. You are all in all, the existence of all, knower of all, and bestower of happiness. You are beyond all phenomena of the universe, untouched by the universe, unattached.

26. O Mother Goddess, again we bow to thee. We pray to thee

from all directions again and again.

27-28. You are form and formless. You are the mother of fulfillment and knowledge, you are the fruit of real *sādhanā*, you are the seeker, you are the adept, and you are the highest of all adepts. Kindly explain everything systematically. Again we bow reverently in front of you.'

29. At the request of the sages, Tripurā, the supreme Mother, the very embodiment of knowledge, spoke compassionately in her clear and authoritative voice.

30. 'Sages, listen to me. I will systematically explain. I will churn the ocean and give the nectar to you.

31-36. This whole universe, like an image in the mirror, is born, it is there, and it annihilates itself. That which is seen by the ignorant as the world is realized by the yogis as pure knowledge. One who is self-delighted and remains calm and undisturbed—great devotees call it one, absolute, and blissful. They worship that supreme Mother according to their knowledge, with pure love and devotion.

That which is the very basis of the senses and internal states, without which nothing exists, and that which is the subject of the scriptures, that self-illumined reality, is my real nature. I am called Tripurā.

37. Far beyond all the worlds there is an ocean of eternal bliss. In the center of that ocean there is an island of gems, and in the midst of that island there is a temple with brilliant illumination. In the inner chamber of that temple is a throne on which is seated Mahātripurāsundarī, the great Mother Divine, with her five aspects. O highest of seers, that is myself.

38-40. Similarly, Sadāśiva, Īśāna, Brahmā, Viṣṇu, Rudra, Gaṇeśa, Skanda, Indra, the goddess of wealth, and other presiding deities who are worthy of worship, as well as the *rākṣasas, devas, nāgas, yakṣas,* and *kinnaras,* are all different aspects of my external nature.

41. In all these aspects, deluded by my own illusion, men

know me not. I am worshiped by all, and I bestow the fruits according to their worship. There is none adored like me, and there is no wish-yielder like me.

42. People receive the fruits according to their *sādhanā.* O seers, my powers are limitless.

43. O seers, I am one, absolute, everlasting, and self-existent reality. I do not need any support, and I am present in all forms of the universe. My light shines forth throughout the universe.

44. By being seen in all the forms of the universe, I do not renounce my true nature. This is the wonder of wonders, which makes the impossible possible.

45. O seers, if you contemplate on my powers, you will know that I am the existence of all. I can be realized, but I am beyond comprehension.

46-47. By my own primal *śakti,* it seems that I am born and will die in the world. Again, it is as though I become the disciple of my *gurudeva,* realize the knowledge of *ātman,* attain freedom, and again and again attain *mokṣa.* Without any help or means, the universe continues to function.

48. In this way my faces are multifarious. Having thousands of eyes, even the *sesa* cannot count my countless powers.

49. Listen, let me give you the essence. From the grain of my power, the world continues to function.

50. According to the philosophy of duality and non-duality, my knowledge varies. According to form and formless, the fruits therein also differ.

51. The philosophies of duality are many because their existence depends on the existence of someone. That is called meditation. Duality is like a dream or a kingdom in the dreaming state.

52. Knowledge bestows duality according to the law of the cycle of providence. Knowledge of the phenomenal world is of various types.

53. As has been said before, the fruit of meditation on Brah-

man is *mokṣa,* but in reality, pure knowledge is called one absolute, without a second.

54. I am beyond and above all, Śrīvidyā. Without pure devotion for a long time, who can attain the knowledge of the absolute?

55. That which is pure, beyond all the phenomenal world, is the knowledge of the absolute, and to contemplate on that is freedom from duality.

56. When the mind and its modifications flow toward the eternal center, *ātman,* O seers, pure *ātman* is realized.

57. By following the sayings of the Vedas and by making sincere efforts, pure *ātman* is known. And when that *ātman* is not identified with the body, it is called real knowledge.

58-59. Real knowledge is that through which duality disappears. By obtaining knowledge of the absolute, nothing remains unattained.

60. O great seers, the knowledge through which all limitations disappear, that alone is the real nature of *ātman.* The same *ātman* is one absolute, without a second.

61. Just as after enlightenment, that ancient, doubtful nature disappears, in exactly the same way the clouds are dispersed by the force of the wind. That is real knowledge.

62. After most of the desires are removed, if any desires exist at all, those desires are harmless, like a snake whose fangs have been broken. That is knowledge beyond.

63. The result of this supreme knowledge bestows freedom from all miseries and makes one fearless. This liberation is the fruit of pure knowledge.

64. Fear has its root in desire. And after attaining the knowledge of one absolute, how is it possible for duality to exist? The moment the sun rises, darkness is dispelled.

65. O seers, after getting freedom from the sense of dualism, fear vanishes. That which does not exist, but seems to exist, causes fear.

66. The acknowledgment of that which is non-existent is subject to destruction. How can you remain fearless in such a state?

67. Meeting ends in parting. Therefore, the fruits received therein also go to decay and destruction.

68-69. If there is anything to be obtained other than *ātman*, then there will be fear. But the realization of that self-existent *ātman* is the state of fearlessness. This state has been called identical with the self by all wise men. That is *mokṣa*. It occurs when the knower, knowledge, and that which is attained become one.

70. Then alone, one is completely free from fear and attains liberation. Also, the entire mind and its modifications, along with shallow knowledge, vanish.

71. The seeker is not aware of his self-existent reality. Gurus and scriptures confirm this reality. There is no other way.

72-74. As long as one is aware of the knower, knowledge, and the means through which it is gained, that is not the state of enlightenment. When the knower becomes aware of his self-existent reality, he is free from the delusion of duality. This is pure knowledge.

75. From the beginning to the end, there is only one self-existent truth. Only for accomplishing worldly duties does there seem to be a diversity. In the beginning and end, one is always one.

76. Because of the veil of maya, ignorance, one *ātman* is seen as the knower, the doer, and the deed. Until the veil lifts, the whole world stands like a huge mountain of obstacles.

77. When the sense of duality created by maya is removed, then the cycle of birth and death vanishes, like clouds dispersed by the wind.

78. For attaining final liberation, all resources should be applied. If all efforts are made, with full compassion and a one-pointed mind, then one does not need any other means.

79. If there is no firm determination, no matter if thousands of means are applied, it will be of no use. Therefore, firm determination is the prime means.

80. "No matter what happens, we have to accomplish it." This determination is the only way. Those who are endowed with this great quality attain freedom.

81. Depending on his strength, purity, and determination, the practitioner attains freedom in a few days, months, or years, or in the next life.

82. There are many impurities in the mind that disturb and defeat the seekers' efforts. Because of this, they are born again and again into this terrible world.

83. The first impurity is lack of faith. The second is the desire to gratify the senses. The third is inertia. In this way, in brief, there are three categories of impurities.

84. There are two types of obstructions. One is doubt and the other is hallucination. The thought "Is there anything like *mokṣa?*" is doubt, the first obstruction.

85. The second obstruction is not acknowledging bondage; therefore freedom is not needed. Both are serious obstructions in *sādhanā.*

86. With firm determination, both of these obstacles can be removed. Complete freedom from them is obtained only when the cause of these obstructions is uprooted. There is no other way.

87-88. Non-belief and thinking contrary to the sayings of the scriptures are the two main causes. If they are discarded and logic is applied according to the scriptures, then this twofold obstruction can be removed. After its removal, firm faith arises. By removing these two barriers, freedom is attained.

89. Desire to enjoy worldly objects creates an obstacle to listening to the teacher, because one whose mind is filled with desire cannot comprehend the truth.

90. When the mind is preoccupied, it is just like being blindfolded. Such a student is always preoccupied with the desired object. He does not see things placed in front of his eyes or hear words spoken into his ears.

91. For one whose mind is filled with the enjoyment of the

objects of the world, listening to the sayings of the scriptures is in vain. With the help of non-attachment, one can control such a mind.

92. There are thousands of impure desires. Strongest among them is *kāma,* the desire to enjoy. After destroying this desire, all impurities are removed.

93. Therefore, with the help of non-attachment, one must eliminate his desire for sense-gratification. The idea "I should possess it" should be eliminated.

94. Desire remains predominant in the objects one can obtain and remains subtle in those which are difficult to obtain. In this way all expectations can be shunned by practicing *vairāgya*, non-attachment.

95. The main cause of desire lies in brooding, with the expectation of obtaining the desired objects. When non-attachment is practiced, such desires are destroyed.

96-97. Inertia is the third impurity of mind. O sages, it is not possible to remove it without the help of practice. Because of inertia, all the potentials of the *sādhakas* are destroyed.

98. To obtain freedom from that inherent inertia, devotion to the absolute alone is the way. Through devotion and dedication, this inherent habit pattern can be modified.

99. If those who suffer on account of this inertia apply all their resources in devotion to the absolute according to their ability, they receive the fruits either in this lifetime or the next.

100-102. All spiritual practices have only one goal, and that is to attain me. One who with pure heart and mind devotes himself to me crosses all barriers and attains bliss. It is I who motivates intelligence. One who, ignoring me, treads the path of spirituality, stumbles at every step. It is not certain that he will receive the fruits of his *sādhanā.*

103-5. Therefore, O seers, the main requirement for *sādhanā* is firm determination, and one who has that is a higher *sādhaka.*

Among them, he who is endowed with devotion toward me is the most revered. Perfection means considering the body to be non-self and centering one's awareness in the self. This is called *siddhi,* perfection.

106. People have not realized their pure self. That is why they are caught in the round of births and deaths and go to their destruction.

107-8. Therefore those practitioners who identify pure consciousness, through which all objects are illumined, alone remove all the impurities. Those purified ones remain absorbed in that realization. Powers such as traveling through space and of attaining *aṇimā siddhi* are not really attainments. That which liberates the aspirant is attainment in reality.

109. All yogic powers are limited by time and place. Therefore they are not even one-sixteenth part of the highest *siddhi,* self-realization.

110. The pure knowledge of *ātman* cannot be divided. They are all segments of the knowledge of *ātman.*

111. Those so-called *siddhis* create obstacles on the path of self-realization. The true seeker does not gain or attain anything, just as no one attains anything from a magician's creation.

112. One for whom even the desire for attaining the highest state has no value, for such a one, what good are these *siddhis,* because they are mere pastimes.

113. There is no *siddhi* superior to self-realization. By this *siddhi* alone man transcends all sorrows and attains perennial bliss.

114-15. Self-realization is the only *siddhi* which leads one beyond the sphere of time. There is no other way. According to the Vedic scriptures, the *sādhanā* for purifying the mind and strengthening the knowledge of consciousness is of three categories: first, second, and third.

116. When one has firm faith and a sharpened intellect, and

has attained deep contemplation, such a one can recite the *śruti* appropriately, though he remains in the midst of worldly activities.

117-19. One who always remains aware of the self amid worldly activities belongs to the second category. One who remains sincerely engaged in Vedic studies and at time's commits mistakes in pronunciation belongs to the third category.

120-21. O seers, ultimately the science of the knowledge of *ātman* is threefold. That knowledge that makes one aware of the real self in all activities is called the first category; that which is maintained only when one is not engrossed in external activities is the second category; and that knowledge which remains only during meditation is the lowest category.

122. When the knowledge of the self exists in the dream and other states, that is the highest.

123. When knowledge of *ātman* exists even as previous *saṁskāras* take their toll, that is the highest.

124. When, without making any effort, the knowledge of self-realization is maintained, that is also the highest.

125. When a man engages in worldly activities and sees the polarities of objects, yet internally remains above all, that means he has attained perfection.

126. Those yogis who in the waking state perform their actions, yet remain completely rested and free from all attachments, are considered to be in the higher state.

127. One with such a *siddhi* is the highest of all seekers. One whose *samādhi* is not disturbed, even while functioning in the external world, is higher than any other seeker.

128. One who has become aware of the level of realization of other seekers is higher than any other seeker.

129. Because of his own self-realization, one who is completely free from doubts and desires is higher than any other seeker.

130. One who does not have even a single doubt or desire and is fearless in functioning in the world is considered by accomplished ones to be higher than any other seeker.

131. One who sees both the bound and liberated individuals in his own self, and thus realizes himself to be *ātman* of all, is higher than any other seeker.

132. One who sees both the ignorant and wise in himself, that realized soul is considered to be higher than any other seeker.

133. One who renounces even the desire for self-realization, and sees both bondage and knowledge within himself, is higher than any other seeker.

134. What to say? I am that accomplished one. There is no difference between him and me. O seers, I have resolved all your questions. If you contemplate on my teaching, you will be free from attachment.'

135. O son of Bhṛgu, saying this, that Mother Divine went into deep silence. By listening to her, the doubts in the minds of all the seers were completely dispelled, and bowing in front of Śiva and other *devas,* the seers happily left for their abodes.

136. I have given you the profound knowledge that dispels the darkness of ignorance. If you assimilate this knowledge and contemplate on it, surely it will lead you to the kingdom of divine bliss.

137-38. This exquisite celestial song was sung by the Mother Divine for the benefit of the seers. Those who daily recite the songs of this scripture with firm faith make her happy, and she imparts pure knowledge to them. To those drowning in the ocean of delusion, this is a safe boat. And to those who are in darkness, this is the light that dispels it."

Thus ends Chapter 20, which is like a perennial song that engulfs all ignorance.

21

The Means of Attaining Knowledge, the Signs of Attainment, and the Dialogue Between Hemāṅgada and the *Brahmarākṣasa*

1. IN THIS WAY Paraśurāma's confusion was almost removed by the teachings of Dattātreya.

2-4. Paying homage to the master, he humbly asked, "O lord, please give me the essence and the exact way of *sādhanā*—that which is simple and direct, bestower of liberation. Also, please tell me the signs and symptoms of the enlightened ones so that I can recognize them immediately."

5-6. Paraśurāma questioned the compassionate Dattātreya, who became very happy and said, "O Paraśurāma, listen. I will tell you the secrets of *sādhanā*.

7-8. The grace of the Lord is the means of attaining knowledge. For that one who with full zeal surrenders himself to the Lord, attaining knowledge becomes certain. Therefore, O Paraśurāma, this is the best way of attaining pure knowledge.

9. Self-surrender is the best of means. Without it, the fruits of pure knowledge cannot be attained. If it is not used, other means do not avail.

10. I will tell you the reason. Knowledge is synonymous with pure consciousness. That illumines all.

11. The imaginary veil around that self-luminous conscious-

ness is removed with the help of contemplation. By having freedom from that, its pure nature is realized.

12. Those *sādhakas* who are involved in worldly activities find it very difficult. Devotees are filled with profound devotion; they are very loyal to their *sādhanā*. That is why they attain higher consciousness easily. This is undoubtedly true.

13-14. If one is devoted to God and simultaneously practices non-attachment and other means, he easily feels oneness with the self. After that, if he shares his knowledge with other worthy *sādhakas*, consciousness of the truth is strengthened.

15-16. In this way, by constant contemplation, one becomes strong enough to receive the grace of Śiva and attains freedom from pain and pleasure. Wherever he travels, he sees Śiva in all. In this way, by being a great adept, he attains the status of *jīvanmukta* and liberates himself in this lifetime.

17-18. Having full reverence toward seekers and discussing the nature of the self with them is higher *sādhanā*. There is no *sādhanā* equal to contemplation with devotion.

19. O Paraśurāma, it is very difficult to know the signs and symptoms of the attained souls, because their true nature is beyond the perception of the senses and beyond the explanation of others.

20. External symptoms are not an indication of the knowledge within. By noticing external symptoms—like physical magnanimity, good garments, and jewels—one can never know how much knowledge of the scriptures another has. Similarly, others cannot know one's state of enlightenment.

21. O Paraśurāma, if one tastes something sweet, he alone experiences the taste. Others do not. Similarly, the knowledge of one person is not known to others.

22. Just as the ants can find their way instinctively, similarly, the wise and learned ones undoubtedly know the realized ones.

23. In the scriptures, tranquility and several other symptoms have been explained. But it is not necessarily true that those

symptoms are found in the liberated ones. There are many gross and subtle symptoms which are not known to ordinary people.

24-25. It is possible for people to imitate the way realized souls speak and act. If those whose inner faculties are not purified practice the technique for attaining knowledge and their minds become steady, they can develop external qualities similar to those of the realized ones. However, their impurities prevent them from attaining permanent spiritual wisdom and bliss.

26. Those who are unaffected by gain and loss, praise and insults, victory and defeat are the higher order of *sādhakas.*

27. Those who spontaneously and confidently come up with answers to any questions related to self-realization are the best *jñānīs.*

28. One who is inspired by hearing about spiritual knowledge and does not hesitate to discuss it is also endowed with the symptoms of a *jñānī.*

29. Those endowed with a content and purified mind, who perform actions selflessly and are tranquil even during great upheavals, are the best *jñānīs.*

30. O Paraśurāma, they have many other characteristics, but remember that the analysis of these qualities is meant for gauging one's own love of spiritual development, not for others.

31-32. The *sādhaka* should always remain engaged in introspection. As one shows great skill in examining others, similarly, if he examines himself attentively within and without, he will surely attain perfection.

33. When the *sādhaka* stops seeing the good and bad qualities of others and starts examining within himself, then he attains *siddhis.*

34. Paraśurāma, the characteristics of the *jñānīs* explained here should be applied only during self-analysis.

35-36. In the examination of others, these standards may not apply. The aspirants who have purified their minds and hearts attain the goal even with their initial effort.

37-38. After attaining the goal, they continue performing actions on the basis of their previous karmas and *saṁskāras.*

How can you recognize those *jñānīs* by observing their activities? Only a *jñānī* can recognize another *jñānī* through his insight, like jewelers alone can test precious gems and know if they are genuine.

39. The lowest level of *jñānīs* seem outwardly similar to the ignorant because they have not yet achieved *sahaja samādhi,* spontaneous *samādhi.*

40. As long as they remain in contemplation they are complete, but the moment they get up, they start identifying themselves with their bodies and experience pain and pleasure just as animals do.

41-43. When two corners of a cloth are dipped in dye, the rest of the material soaks up the dye. Just so, a worldly experience occurring during contemplation is colored by contemplative truth. That is why it cannot become a cause of bondage.

44. During contemplation, though he functions in the world, his awareness of the self exists. That is why he is not in bondage.

45. The second category of *jñānīs* do not identify themselves with their bodies. The wise remain eternally aware of the self.

46-47. When they are in a state of *samādhi* they cannot participate in any external activities. As in the sleeping state the body's natural functions continue, so is the case in *samādhi.* A person may speak or act in sleep due to his previous *vāsanās,* but he is not aware of it.

48-49. A drunk does not remember what he said or did. Likewise, if by chance a great yogi of this intermediate stage performs actions, he does so without being aware of them.

50-51. Because of the karmas of his past lives, his body is sustained. But the highest *jñānīs* do not have body-awareness. Just as the charioteer drives the chariot, the chariot of the body is also driven.

52. As the charioteer driving the chariot does not identify

himself with the chariot, similarly an adept does not identify himself with his body and its functions, and he has no consciousness of his own body. Such a one is fully realized.

53. Pure from within, established in *ātman*-consciousness, he acts in the world exactly the way a man in a drama dresses as a woman and assumes the part.

54. While playing with a child, a mature person behaves like a child, yet is unaffected by the result of the game; similarly, the highest-level *jñānī* functions in the world yet remains unaffected.

55. A second-level *jñānī* maintains his spiritual awareness with the help of control over the mind and its modifications, but such a *jñānī*'s attainment is due to his firmness.

56. The *jñānīs* are in three categories on the basis of their maturity and stability. In this regard, I will narrate a dialogue between two enlightened ones. Please listen.

57-58. Long ago in a mountainous region there lived a king named Ratnāṅgada. He lived in the city Amṛta near the bank of the Vipasa River. He had two sons, Rukmāṅgada and Hemāṅgada, who were very brilliant and were the favorites of their father.

59. The older prince, Rukmāṅgada, was an authority on the scriptures, while the younger one, Hemāṅgada, was a *jñānī* of the highest caliber, a knower of the self.

60-61. One fine spring day they rode into the dense forest with their army to hunt deer. They shot deer, tigers, rabbits, and wild buffalo. Exhausted at last, they sat down near a lake.

62. On the other side of the lake a *brahmarākṣasa* (a brahmin ghost) was living in a banyan tree. He was an excellent scholar, who would challenge other savants to philosophical debates.

63-67. He would eat his defeated opponents. He lived like this for a long time. The senior prince also had a penchant for debate. When he heard about the learned *brahmarākṣasa* he went to see him and launched into an argument. When the younger prince saw that his brother was defeated and was about to be carried off by the *brahmarākṣasa*, he cried, 'O *brahmarākṣasa*, do not eat him yet! I am his younger brother. Defeat me also and then you can eat us both.' Hearing this proposal, the *brahmarākṣasa* replied, 'I am starving to death! It has been ages since my last meal! I will eat him first, and then debate with you.

68-69. O prince, I am quite sure that once I defeat and devour you, I will be fully satisfied! The sage Vasiṣṭha gave me a boon. Many years ago his disciple Devarāta came here, and I ate him, too. Then Vasiṣṭha cursed me,

70-71. "O *brahmarākṣasa,* from this day forth, if you eat human flesh, your face will be burned!" When I begged for mercy, he granted this boon:

72. "You may eat only those human beings you have defeated in debate." I have always obeyed his injunction.

73. Finally I have won this delicious morsel. O prince, after eating him, I will debate with you.'

74-75. Saying this, he was ready to eat the elder prince. The younger prince interrupted, 'O *brahmarākṣasa,* please hear my request. Tell me, is there anything you will take from me in exchange for my brother?'

76. Hearing this, the *brahmarākṣasa* replied, 'Listen, prince. There is nothing for which I can exchange him.

77-78. Who would give up a delicious meal after going hungry for so long? However, there is one possibility. I have some questions. If you can answer them, I will free your brother.'

79-80. The prince said, 'Ask. I will reply.'

'What is wider than space and subtler than an atom? What is its nature, and where does it exist?'

81. 'O *brahmarākṣasa,* listen. *Cit,* absolute consciousness, is larger than space and more subtle than an atom. Its nature is self-luminous and it abides in the self.'

82. 'O prince, if it is one and at the same time all-pervading, then how can it be the most subtle? What is that illumination and what is the self?'

83. 'As the cause of all, it extends everywhere. It cannot be perceived by the senses, therefore it is subtle, too. Both light and self are identical with consciousness.'

84. 'Where does the place exist where consciousness can be attained, and what happens after attaining it?'

85. 'O *brahmarākṣasa,* listen. *Buddhi,* pure mind, and one-pointedness is that through which consciousness is attained. Once it is attained, one is not reborn.'

86. 'O prince, what is *buddhi* and how does one make it one-pointed? How is it born? What is birth?'

87. 'Consciousness veiled by ignorance is called *buddhi.* One-pointedness means uninterrupted contemplation on *ātman.* To identify with the body causes birth.'

88. 'Why is consciousness not attained? What is the way of attaining it? Why is one born?'

89. 'O *Brahmarākṣasa,* listen. Because of ignorance it is not attained. It is attained spontaneously. Birth is the result of thinking one is the doer.'

90. 'O prince, what is that ignorance? What is the real self? What is the sense of doership?'

91. 'Listen, *brahmarākṣasa.* To identify the self with the body is ignorance. What is the nature of *ātman*? Ask yourself from where the sense "I do it" arises. This desire brings you back as a doer, and such a desire is the ego of the doer.'

92. 'O prince, how can ignorance be dispelled? What is its cause, and what is at the root of that cause?'

93. 'O *brahmarākṣasa,* listen. It is overcome through *vicāra,* right contemplation. The cause of *vicāra* is *vairāgya,* non-attachment. And the cause of non-attachment is acknowledging the impermanence of worldly objects.'

94. 'O prince, what is that contemplation? What is non-attachment, and what is a negative attitude toward the objects of the world?'

95. 'Discrimination of the non-self from the self is called contemplation. Complete indifference to the objects of the world is called non-attachment. Objects create pain because of one's negative attitude toward them.'

96. 'How can these means be attained? And what is the root cause of that?'

97. 'Listen, *brahmarākṣasa.* All this is possible only through the grace of God, and that is obtained through pure devotion. Pure devotion is received from *satsaṅga,* the company of the sages.'

98. 'O prince, tell me: What is God? What is devotion? Who are called sages?'

99. 'Listen, O *Brahmarākṣasa.* One who sustains the universe is God, and meditating on that is called *bhakti,* devotion. Those who are tranquil and merciful are called sages.'

100. 'O prince, tell me: Who is always fearful and miserable? Who always suffers from poverty?'

101. 'Those who are extremely rich are always fearful. Those who have a large family are miserable. Those who are entangled in the snare of expectations are always poor.'

102. 'O prince, tell me. Who can be fearless in the world? Who is free from sorrow?'

103. 'Listen, O *Brahmarākṣasa.* A man who is non-attached is fearless. One who has perfect control over the mind is free from grief. And one who has known that which is to be known is free from poverty.'

104. 'O prince, tell me who is that one who can be recognized with great difficulty? Who does not have body-consciousness, yet lives? What is called the non-doer state of life?'

105. 'O *brahmarākṣasa,* a *jīvanmukta,* one who is liberated here and now, is hard to recognize. Since he does not identify with it, he is free from the body but still has a body. He performs all actions while remaining internally inactive. He performs actions yet remains untouched.'

106. 'What is existent, and what is not existent? What is

impossible? After you have answered this, I will release your brother.'

107. 'O *Brahmarākṣasa,* the eternal seer, pure consciousness, cannot be perceived. Therefore, there is no activity in it. Now I have answered your questions. Release my brother immediately.'

108. Having heard this, the *brahmarākṣasa* became very happy and released Rukmāṅgada. Then he assumed his previous state of brahminhood.

109. Seeing this transformation of the brahmin, the princes wondered and asked, 'Who are you?'

110. Then that wise brahmin explained all about his past. 'I was a famous brahmin in the kingdom of Magadha.

111-12. I was famous as Vasumān and was well versed in all the scriptures. I was proud of my learning and I defeated hundreds of learned brahmins in debates many times. I became very egotistical.

113. I always remained eager to learn the scriptures and was brilliant in using logic. Once while discussing the existence of *ātman,* I encountered the sage Aṣṭaka in a debate held by the King of Magadha. He was a tranquil seer.

114-15. In the debate, I used mere logic and opposed him fiercely. Though his answers were appropriate and full of authoritative references, with the help of my crafty logic, again and again I dispersed all his arguments.

116. In that debate, he was very calm. Kaśyapa, a disciple of that great sage, got angry and cursed me.

117. "O egotistical brahmin, you are insulting my *gurudeva* for no rhyme or reason. Therefore, you will become a brahmin ghost for a long time."

118. I was terrified at being cursed like this and sought refuge in the sage Aṣṭaka, bowing in front of him.

119. The sage remained tranquil and though I was his opponent, he was kind to me. He put a time limit on the curse.

120-21. The sage said, "Whatever questions you have asked

were resolved by me, yet you obstinately used logic. The day a learned man resolves all your questions, you will be free from the curse."

122. O prince, many years have elapsed. Now you have freed me from that curse. Therefore I admit that you are king of kings and the leader among *jñānīs.*'

123. The prince was astonished to hear this. Again that brahmin questioned him and again his questions were resolved by the prince. After giving due reverence to the brahmin, the prince and his elder brother returned to their city with their platoon of soldiers."

124. Sage Dattātreya said, "O Paraśurāma, I have answered all the queries you have raised."

Thus ends Chapter 21, containing the dialogue between the brahmarākṣasa and the prince.

22

The Resolution of Vasumān's Questions and the Summary of the Scripture

1. AFTER LISTENING TO THE STORY of the *brahmarākṣasa,* Paraśurāma asked his master, Dattātreya, with great reverence,

2. "Lord, what did that brahmin ask after he was freed from the curse and what was Hemāṅgada's answer? Kindly let me know.

3. I am curious. It could not have been a mere debate."

At his request, the compassionate Dattātreya replied,

4. "Paraśurāma, that dialogue was profound and deep. I will tell you. Vasumān asked the prince, who was sitting nearby,

5. 'Prince, I want to ask something. Can you please explain? In the beginning, I received this knowledge from the sage Aṣṭāvakra.

6. After hearing you, I now understand how to attain the highest state of knowledge.

7. How can a person who has known what ought to be known continue interacting with the world? It is like the co-existence of darkness and light.

8. Prince, please explain the reason clearly.'

At his request the prince spoke,

9. 'O brahmin, your confusion is not yet completely removed.

How can the knowledge identical with one's own self be negated by worldly activity?

10. If knowledge can be negated by living in the world, then that knowledge is no more valuable than a dream.

11. All worldly activity has its basis in knowledge, so how can knowledge be negated? Please tell me.

12. Knowledge is that through which the entire universe is seen. Through *saṅkalpa,* firm determination, all worldly activities seem to appear within knowledge itself.

13. When one becomes desireless and knows *ātman,* then the individual soul attains freedom from all bondage and enjoys happiness.

14. O brahmin, therefore, your question is invalidated by wise men.' Then Vasumān said to the kind-hearted prince,

15. 'Sir, this is true. I have arrived at the same conclusion myself. Pure consciousness is called pure knowledge.

16. After attaining enlightenment and experiencing pure consciousness, if someone still has desires, he will still be deluded, exactly the way a rope can be mistaken for a snake. Mistaken identity is illusion.'

17-18. The prince replied, 'Brahmin, listen. You do not know how to distinguish confusion from non-confusion. Those who know the sky is colorless still perceive it as blue and use the words "The sky is blue." The fact that they see and speak this way does not mean that they have any illusions about the color of the sky.

19. To the ignorant, it is confusion, whereas to the knower of the truth, it is not. A realized person's knowledge cannot be the source of bondage any more than a dead snake can bite.

20. There is certainly a difference between the worldly interactions and behaviors of a *jñānī* and an ignorant person. The *jñānī's* interactions with the world are like images in a mirror.

21. In the case of a *jñānī,* the knowledge related to his dealings with the world is valid; while in the case of an ignorant

person, it is otherwise. All of a *jñānī's* activities are based on knowledge.

22. Because *jñānīs* are constantly aware that all actions and interactions with the world are like images reflecting in a mirror, they are free from ignorance.

23. That which is born out of ignorance can be dispelled by knowledge. That which is born out of ignorance cannot furnish the means of attaining knowledge.

24. That is why a diseased person has double vision. This world is seen as it is because of past karmas. All the experiences of the world come from one's own karmas.

25. Therefore, as long as those karmas and their subtle impressions are not destroyed, interaction with the world continues. The moment all karmas are exhausted, there exists only pure consciousness.

26. Thus confusion can never arise from pure knowledge.'

Hearing this, the brahmin asked the prince,

27. 'O prince, how can action possibly be performed by a *jñānī*? How is a *jñānī* able to perform actions when the fire of knowledge burns all karmas?'

28-29. The prince replied, 'Brahmin, there are three kinds of karmas: *apakva* (unripe), *pakva* (ripe), and *hatodita* (destroyed before they germinate). For *jñānīs*, all karmas are destroyed except for the ripe ones.

30-31. Providence or nature (*niyati*) has appointed time as the ripener. The karmas that are ripe are called *pakva*. *Apakva* karmas are not yet ripe. The karmas that are performed after self-realization are not binding.

32. Ripe karmas are also called *prārabdha* karmas. They are like arrows already sent toward their target. They keep moving toward their target until the force impelling them is exhausted.

33. The experience of worldly phenomena continues for the *jñānī* because of his resulting karma; but his response depends on the degree of his knowledge. The *jñānī* still undergoes the results

of his previous actions; his reaction to them depends on his degree of realization.

34-35. For the lowest-level *jñānī,* the result of karma is instant and very clear. For the second-level *jñānī,* karmic fruits are insignificant. The highest *jñānī,* however, remains unaffected by the fruits of his karma, for he knows that it is not any more real than a rabbit's horns. That is why the highest *jñānīs* are said to be free from the bondage of karma.

36. Prior to the performance of an action, the ignorant anticipate the entire sequence and its consequences. That is how they bind themselves with the strands of karma.

37. The lowest-level *jñānī* makes an effort to contemplate the self, so his preoccupation with the results of his actions is broken from time to time. For this reason, the results of his karma are not very powerful.

38. The middle-level *jñānī* experiences the results of his ripe karmas like a person in deep sleep experiences a mosquito bite. The discomfort is minimal.

39. However, for the highest type of *jñānī,* even the full fruits of his actions are like nothing at all, for they have been burnt by the fire of knowledge. For him, those karmas lose their binding power.

40-41. Like an actor performing in a drama who plays his role without being affected by the sorrow or delight he expresses on the stage, the highest *jñānī* remains unaffected by even the full effect of his ripe karma. Therefore, his karmic fruit is as illusory as the horn of a rabbit.

42. The ignorant do not have pure knowledge of *ātman.* Therefore they identify themselves with their bodies, considering worldly objects as real.

43-46. The lowest level of *jñānīs* have realized the self and have also understood the unreality of the external world, but they lack sufficient practice and identify their bodies with the self because their knowledge is clouded by the impurities of their past karmas. That is why on and off they think the world is real. Then again, knowledge comes forward and dispels the darkness of ignorance. Thus, *saṁskāras* and knowledge mingle and make them reap the fruits of past actions.

47. O brahmin, knowledge mingled with *saṁskāras* has quite different fruits and they are not equally effective. Desire for knowledge is good; therefore, it makes one aware of the desire for those objects that create obstacles. These obstacles cannot obstruct the desire for attaining truth.

48-49. Under the influence of false desire, the seeker forgets the desire for truth. That false desire can be renounced with firm determination and then he gains a pure desire to attain truth. After this, that powerful desire for obtaining truth never becomes an obstacle.

50. In the case of a second-level *jñānī,* the truth is never forgotten and false knowledge vanishes. He performs his actions in the world, while maintaining his awareness.

51-52. This state is a state of the second level of adept. Now I will tell you about the seekers. When a seeker starts treading the path of *ātman,* his awareness begins to strengthen. When this awareness is completely strengthened, he can never forget his true nature. Without firm determination, the false appearance of duality cannot be removed.

53. O brahmin, seen from the standpoint of a completely realized one, there is no difference between *samādhi* and the activities of the world. One who has attained *samādhi* is always aware of the truth.

54-55. The second level of aspirant who has attained *samādhi* is sometimes not aware of his true self. When he encounters false knowledge, he becomes weaker. But one who is of the highest level of *jñānīs* remains tranquil at all times because his awareness is firmly established, even when he is not in *samādhi.*

56. O brahmin, listen. Actually for both the middle- and highest-level *jñānīs* the effects of the karmas are not very significant,

because these *jñānīs* have attained perfection. They see nothing except the self.

57. When all their karmas are burnt by the fire of knowledge, then no karma remains to be performed.

58. Like a magician, the things they do are just shows put on for the sake of others. O brahmin, I am going to briefly tell you the secret.

59. The highest-level *jñānīs'* awareness is like the awareness of Śiva. There is no difference at all. This is the truth.

60-61. Therefore, all the karmas of the highest-level *jñānīs* are exhausted.'

After Prince Hemāṅgada's explanation, the brahmin's doubt was dispelled and he was illumined within. He went to his kingdom happily.

62. After this, both princes returned to their capital."

Hearing this, Paraśurāma asked Dattātreya,

63. "O *gurudeva,* I heard these wise words from your mouth. My doubts are dispelled and at last I comprehend the knowledge of the absolute reality.

64-65. All-pervading *ātman* is seen throughout the universe. O *gurudeva,* please summarize everything you have told me once more so that I can keep the essence intact in my heart."

66. At his request Dattātreya said, "Paraśurāma, listen. I will give you the essence.

67-68. The supreme Mother of the universe is pure consciousness. Her very being is the experience of pure "I-am-ness." Through her power of sovereignty she lets the impossible become possible, and thus allows this universe to appear within herself like images in a mirror. Listen to how she manifests this universe.

69. Because of her essential experience of pure I-am-ness, pure consciousness is all-pervading. Then in the beginning, through her power of sovereignty, she lets herself appear to be twofold.

70-71. One aspect of her appears as pure "I-ness," while the other aspect is devoid of the sense of self, and appears as matter. O Paraśurāma, the external aspect is called "matter," and the aspect that appears as "I-ness" is called Sadāśiva.

72. Although the formless, absolute, self-existent, unmanifest sees that material part as something separate from himself, he still experiences it as the self.

73. He, again through his *svātantrya śakti* [willpower], desires to manifest the universe and begins considering *avyakta,* the unmanifest, to be his body ('I am this'), and starts believing it.

74. During his experimentation, Sadāśiva became Īśvara. That which uses ego as its instrument is called Īśvara.

75. Īśvara, who is in fact the experience of the entire unmanifest world, then becomes threefold: Rudra (the annihilator), Viṣṇu (the preserver), and Brahmā (the creator).

76-77. There have been numerous Brahmās, Viṣṇus, and Rudras. That is what providence is.

78-79. O Paraśurāma, it is like the image in a mirror. Nothing is real. Pure consciousness is always experiencing her perfect "I-awareness." It is immovable, but because of its ego ('I-ness'), it seems as though it moves.

80. O Paraśurāma, you pervade your whole body and call it "I." Aware of "your" different senses and limbs and actions, through them, you feel you are the doer.

81. Likewise, pure consciousness is the center of pure "I-amness," and experiences the entire manifestation, from the highest Sadāśiva to the grossest elements. Pure consciousness, which is also the foundation of ego-centered awareness, is seen as the cause of illumination.

82-84. You cannot experience, smell, taste, or touch sense-objects while maintaining awareness of pure "I." You can experience them only by identifying yourself with the senses. Just so, Sadāśiva is identical with Brahmā, Rudra, and everything down to the material elements. He is aware of his oneness with everything and performs all actions in the universe through his instruments, Brahmā, Viṣṇu, and other deities.

85-86. Just as your *nirvikalpa* state of being is the very foundation of all, O Paraśurāma, that real perfect one is neither doer nor knower. Likewise, the supreme consciousness, although the source of all, knows no duality and initiates no activity. The entire illusory universe appears in her.

87-88. Through her supreme power, she seems to appear like the images in a mirror. Therefore, the universe is no more different from her than a reflection from a mirror. You and I and all perceivers are actually pure consciousness, as long as we do not identify ourselves with external objects.

89. A mirror with many reflecting images appears to have many sections, but when all objects are removed, the reflections also disappear; then the mirror alone remains.

90. Likewise, after the appearance of duality is removed, pure consciousness alone remains. Just as an image is seen in a jar of water, similarly, an image is seen in the mirror of pure consciousness.

91. That state of freedom is pure consciousness, the absolute state. There is no sorrow in it; therefore, it is full of everlasting bliss.

92. Because that state is essentially bliss, everyone desires to attain it. The very nature of the self is joy. That is why all individuals long to realize it.

93. Because of the presence of the self in the body, the body is dear to all; bodily joys are called worldly pleasures.

94. In deep sleep, when one's awareness is not identified with objects, bliss alone is experienced. Consciousness is full of bliss and everyone wants to attain it.

95. The ignorant are not aware of the bliss attained from *ātman*. They think that happiness can be found in external ob-

jects. That is why they consider happiness to be different from the self.

96-98. As long as one does not realize he is looking into a mirror, the images reflecting on it seem real. But the moment the reflections are removed, one definitely knows the mirror is pure. He also knows that the mirror is unaffected by those reflections. Likewise, a *jñānī* knows that *ātman* alone exists in everyone, and there is nothing beyond it.

99. This universe appears in the self just as a clay pot appears in clay, ornaments in gold, and statues in rock.

100. O Paraśurāma, whoever claims, 'This universe does not exist,' is mistaken, because the idea that it does not exist cannot be proven through any source of valid knowledge.

101-2. By the negation of duality and the idea that 'It does not exist,' there is only self-existent consciousness, which witnesses both. How can it be proven that the universe does not exist? As a city is seen in a mirror, in the same way, the whole universe rests in pure consciousness.

103-4. This is perfect knowledge because it is not opposed by any opposite concept. Through its power of sovereignty, consciousness seems to exist as the universe, just as the image of a city appears in a mirror. This is the essence of the scriptures.

105-6. There is no bondage; there is no liberation. There is no aspirant, and there is no way of enlightenment. There is only one absolute, self-illumined power of powers. She is seen as ignorance, knowledge, bondage, freedom, and the way of freedom. O Paraśurāma, it is essential to know this. There is nothing else to be known.

107. In this way, from beginning to end, I have systematically imparted the knowledge of attaining truth to you. After realizing this truth, man never grieves.

108-9. Having received the profound knowledge, if a man does not become tranquil, he is like a statue made of stone, and there is no possibility for him to attain knowledge.

110. By hearing this once, knowledge is strengthened, but those who are not very sharp—how will they grasp it, even by listening to it two or three times?

111. This scripture gives one freedom from all sins and leads to a state of tranquility. It is a source of knowledge. It removes all impurities. It purifies the mind. If it is contemplated upon, it gives freedom from the bondage of ignorance.

112. If one contemplates that which is the self-existent *ātman* with a purified mind, he attains *mokṣa.* Otherwise, it is all bondage. That bestower of knowledge is called Tripurā."

Thus Chapter 22 ends happily with a summary of the entire scripture of Tripurā Rahasya.

GLOSSARY

advaita Non-dual; the absolute reality that transcends the objective world; a system of philosophy that expounds the theory of absolute Brahman.

āgamas Revealed tantric texts; tantric texts that have no author.

Agni Fire.

ahambhāva The sense of "I am"; ego; "I am-ness"; individuated consciousness.

ahaṅkāra Ego; the faculty of mind through which one identifies one's self with external objects.

ajapā japa Constant, effortless repetition of one's mantra; japa of "sohum" or any given mantra.

anāhata The unstruck sound; the eternal sound which vibrates without being produced by any source; also refers to the heart center.

Angirā One of the seven primordial sages.

aṇimā siddhi The yogic accomplishment of becoming small at will.

antaḥkaraṇa The inner instruments; i.e., mind, ego, and intellect.

aṇu The smallest unit of matter; an atom; the state of matter that cannot be further divided.

anvaya vyatireka To reach a conclusion through deductive reasoning.

apakva Not ripe; refers to those karmas that have not yet started to produce their fruits, but still exist in seed form.

aparādha vāsanā Skepticism; mental impurity because of which a person doubts, argues, and even rejects the truth.

arhata Literally, qualified ones or accomplished ones; accomplished *sādhakas;* monks of the Jaina order.

ashram Center of learning; a spiritual and educational institution.

Aṣṭaka A sage, probably Aṣṭāvakra, the son of Kahola.

Asthira The unsteady one; mind.

aśvamedha A religious ceremony usually performed by an emperor whose power and authority was respected by other kings. It involved releasing a horse to roam freely throughout all kingdoms as a token of his unsurpassed ruling power. When the horse returns, the ceremony is concluded. This is considered to be very auspicious for the one who sponsors the ceremony.

ātman The center of pure consciousness; self; soul.

Atri One of the seven primordial sages; the father of the sage Dattātreya.

avidyā Ignorance; limited knowledge; the indescribable force that veils the awareness of the true self.

avyakta The unmanifest, primordial nature; also known as *prakṛti.*

bhakti Love and devotion; the path of total surrender and faith.

Bharata An ancient king of India who realized the emptiness of the charms and temptations of worldly objects and renounced the world in the pursuit of self-realization. A detailed account of his life and *sādhanā* can be found in the highly acclaimed scripture *Śrī Madbhāgavatam.*

Bhasmāsura A demon who, through his intense *tapas* and devotion, pleased Śiva and received a boon from him. The boon was that the head of anyone the demon touched would be burned to ashes. After receiving the boon, he tested its power on Śiva. Śiva fled, but the demon chased him. Finally Viṣṇu rescued Śiva by making Bhasmāsura touch his own head. The demon was destroyed and Śiva learned a valuable lesson.

Bhramapurī The city of knowledge; the city where everyone attained the knowledge of Brahman.

Bhṛgu One of the seven primordial sages; the sage who was born from the mind of Brahmā.

Brahmaloka The realm of highest reality.

brahmarākṣasa Unembodied beings who can become visible at will; they either had knowledge of the truth intellectually but did not practice what they knew or, in most cases, are such beings who committed an unforgivable offense and were cursed to live unembodied until they completed their penance.

brahmin The intellectual class in Vedic society; a person who is supposed to know the Vedas.

buddhi The intellect; faculty of discrimination; the aspect of mind that judges, decides, and discriminates.

cakra Wheel; the wheel of life; a center of consciousness; in yogic literature, there are said to be seven *cakras* along the spinal column.

Candramā A sage, the son of Atri.

Capalā The ever-changing, unpredictable figment of the mind; imagination.

cit Consciousness.

cit-śakti The power of consciousness.

citta The mindfield or unconscious mind.

Cyavana A *brahma ṛṣi* who married princess Sukanyā. He is famous for reversing his aging process. His life and accomplishments are recorded in great detail in the highly acclaimed scripture *Śrī Maddevībhāgavatam*.

Dakṣa A son of Brahmā who was one of the *prajāpati* and father of Śakti, Śiva's wife.

Dattātreya The son of the sage Atri and the teacher of the sage Paraśurāma.

deva A bright being; a celestial being.

Devala One of the accomplished yogis; a great saint and yogi who, due to his yogic accomplishment, is known as Yogi Yogeśvara, the Lord of yoga science.

devī Divine Mother; synonymous with Śakti.

dīkṣā Initiation; to officially receive spiritual instruction, most significantly guidance in the practice of a mantra received directly from a teacher.

Durvāsā The son of the sage Atri and the brother of Dattātreya.

dvaita Duality; the system of philosophy that expounds the existence of consciousness and matter as two distinct aspects of reality.

gandharva The category of beings who can be seen only at their will and are supposed to be expert musicians.

Gaṇeśa The son of Śakti and Śiva; the remover of all obstacles.

Gautama A famous sage and the seer of many Vedic mantras.

guru Teacher; a spiritual preceptor; the one who dispels the darkness of ignorance; synonymous with *gurudeva.*

Hāritāyana A disciple of the sage Paraśurāma; the sage who recited the *Tripurā Rahasya* to Nārada.

hatodita Literally, "born dead"; stillborn karmas; karmas that cannot produce fruits because they are performed by an enlightened one.

Hiraṇyagarbha The golden egg; the cosmic "I-ness."

Indra King of gods.

Īśāna Another name for Śiva.

Īśvara God.

jaḍaśakti Unconscious primordial nature; another term for *prakṛti.*

jaḍasamādhi Deep sleep.

Janaka An enlightened king who ruled the kingdom of Mithila and was famous for his spiritual achievement while still living in the world; it was in his assembly that the sage Aṣṭāvakra and the sage Tāpasī had a profound discussion on spirituality.

jivanmukta One who is liberated here and now.

Jñānakhaṇḍa The canto on the knowledge of *Tripurā Rahasya.* It is the third of three cantos, the first being the *Māhātmyakhaṇḍa* and the second, the *Caryākhaṇḍa.* The second canto has been lost.

jñanī An enlightened person; literally, one who has knowledge; these enlightened ones may also be liberated, although many are not.

Jvālāmukha Literally, the one with a fiery mouth; anger, the son of mind.

Kailāsa The abode of Śiva.

kalā The intrinsic power of absolute and omniscient truth through which truth veils its absoluteness and omniscience; the power which creates the illusion that the indivisible truth has divisions and consists of parts.

kāla Time; the unseen factor that leads one through the process of change.

kāma vāsanā Desire for sensory pleasure; false sense of duty; the hidden desires that motivate one to undertake certain actions.

Kaṇva One of the *brahma ṛṣis* present in Brahmaloka during the discussion on the highest reality.

kapha Phlegm; the watery energy.

karma Action; includes the process of performing actions, creating subtle impressions, and later reaping the fruits.

karma vāsanā Subtle impressions of the past which cloud the mind and motivate one to repeat the action in the present.

kartavyaśeṣa The feeling of obligation that is the motivation for undertaking a task.

Kaśyapa A famous sage, the son of Mārīci.

kaula A particular school of tantra which teaches how to use external objects for spiritual unfoldment; a tantric school where wine, meat, fish, physical gesture, and physical union are used as part of the practice.

Kauśika A yogi in the lineage of the sage Viśvāmitra.

kinnara A race of legendary beings who were semi-human; they appear in the *Rāmāyaṇa* and in many other Paurāṇic texts.

Kratu One of the seven primordial sages.

kṣatriya The warrior class.

kundalini śakti The divine force which, according to yogis, remains dormant at the base of the spine and which, through yoga practices, can be awakened and raised all the way to the highest *cakra* where this *śakti* unites with the supreme Śiva.

Lakṣmī The goddess of wealth and prosperity.

Likhita One of the *brahma ṛṣis* present in Brahmaloka during the discussion on the highest reality.

Mahādeva The great bright being; another name for Śiva.

mahā maya The intrinsic power of Brahman; the force through which the one, single, absolute truth manifests into many.

Mahāśanā The one with great appetite, the great eater; expectation; the one who can never be satisfied.

mahāśūnya The great void; the highest state of reality according to Buddhists.

Māhātmyakhaṇḍa The first canto of *Tripurā Rahasya* which describes the glory of the Divine Mother and gives a detailed description of the seekers who followed this path and their experiences.

Mahātripurasundarī The great Divine Mother, Tripurā Sundarī; another name for Tripurā or Śrīvidyā.

mahāvedha The great penetration; the highest kind of initiation that is given by an adept yogi to a fully prepared student; this particular type of initiation is unique in the Śrīvidyā tradition.

mahāvidyā The great wisdom; in the path of *śakti sādhanā* there are ten *mahāvidyās:* Kālī, Tārā, Tripurā, Bhairavī, Bhuvaneśvarī, Bagalāmukhī, Chinnamastā, Mātaṅgī, Kamalā, and Dhūmāvatī.

Maheśa Śiva.

Maheśvara The great Lord; usually another name for Śiva, although it is also used interchangeably for the highest reality—the Divine Mother, Tripurā.

mandala Another word for *yantra;* in tantra *sādhanā* geometrical figures used as symbols for the deities.

mantra The divine words heard by a *ṛṣi* in his or her deep meditation; the spiritual words a student receives from the teacher through initiation.

mantra japa Repetition of mantra.

Mārīca The demon who deceived Rāma by assuming the form of a deer, thus luring him away from Sītā.

maya The power that measures the unmeasurable; the power though which the absolute and unitary consciousness polarizes itself into consciousness and unconscious matter.

medhāvin One who has intuitive wisdom.

miśra The tantric school which stresses the equal importance of external worship and internal meditation.

moha Attachment; delusion.

mokṣa Liberation.

muladhara The root *cakra;* the center of the earth element located at the base of the spine.

nāga Snake; a particular clan or race of people.

Nārada A celestial sage; the sage who first heard the *Tripurā Rahasya* from the sage Hāritāyana.

Nindyavṛtta The corrupt one; negativity.

nirvikalpa samādhi The highest state of *samādhi;* spiritual absorption, where the seeds of all previous *saṁskāras* are completely burnt.

niyati Providence; the force that allows the individual karmas to sprout at a certain time and place.

Nṛsiṁha An incarnation of Viṣṇu, in which he assumed a form half human, half lion.

pakva Karmas which are ripening now and thus affect the present.

parakāyā praveśa vijñāna The science of casting off one's body and entering another body consciously.

Parāśara A *brahma ṛṣi* and father of the famous sage Vyāsa.

Paraśurāma Disciple of the sage Dattātreya; the sage who received the knowledge of Tripurā and taught it to Hāritāyana.

Pāśupata A subdivision of Śaivism.

pitta Bile; fiery energy.

Pracāra The constant traveler in the city of life; here it refers to *prāṇa,* the vital energy that constantly travels through and nourishes the body.

pradhāna Another term for *prakṛti.*

prakṛti Primordial nature; the ultimate cause of the material world.

prāṇa The vital force that nourishes both body and mind; the energy that keeps body and mind together and keeps one alive.

praṇāyāma The restraint of *prāṇa;* breathing exercise.

prārabdha The karmas that have begun producing their fruits; the karmas that have begun manifesting in the form of destiny.

Pulaha One of the seven primordial sages.

Pulastya One of the seven primordial sages.

pūrṇāhantā Perfect "I-ness"; cosmic self-awareness.

puruṣa Consciousness, inner self.

rāga Attachment.

rajas The force that motivates one to perform actions; the force that makes one feel agitated, hyperactive, and full of desires; this kind of energy is called *rajasic.*

rākṣasa A demon.

ṛṣi A seer; a sage.

Rudra Another name for Śiva, especially the aspect that destroys the world or those tendencies that force the human being to remain caught in the worldly net.

Sadāśiva The immortal, eternal Śiva; the one endowed with the power of knowledge who thus bestows his blessings in the form of liberation.

sādhaka An aspirant, a seeker.

sādhanā Spiritual discipline.

Śaivism The philosophy or path of spirituality that leads to the realization of Śiva.

Śaivites Followers of Śaivism.

Śakti The Divine Mother, the highest reality, the vibrant self-conscious energy through which this whole universe evolves.

śaktipāta The bestowing of spiritual energy.

śakti sādhanā Spiritual discipline that leads an aspirant to the realization of Śakti, the divine force within.

Śaktism The philosophy or path of spirituality which proposes the supremacy of Śakti.

samādhi The state of mind that is free from all thought constructs; the state of spiritual absorption in which all questions are fully answered.

samaya The school of tantra which is purely yogic and leads an aspirant to the realization of unitary consciousness.

saṁskāra The subtle impression of our actions stored in the unconscious mind.

saṅkalpla śakti The power of determination.

Śaṅkar Another name for Śiva.

Śaṅkha A *brahma ṛṣi* present in Brahmaloka when the Divine Mother, Tripurā, appeared and imparted the highest knowledge.

sārikā A myna bird.

śāstras Scriptures; the original text on *sādhanā*.

satsaṅga The company of the wise.

sattva The illuminating force; uplifting energy.

Satyaloka The realm of pure truth; the same as Brahmaloka.

savikalpa samādhi A state of spiritual absorption in which the seeds of previous karmas still exist.

siddhi Yogic accomplishments; the unfoldment of human potential through yogic practices.

Śiva The auspicious one; the god of destruction; the light of knowledge which dispels the darkness of ignorance.

Skanda The son of Lord Śiva, also known as Kumāra.

Soma Another name of the sage Candramā, the son of Atri; the moon; the juice of an herb that the Vedic sages used to offer in the fire during their rituals.

śraddha Firm conviction.

Śrīvidyā Another term for Tripurā.

śruti That which is heard; revealed scriptures; the Vedas.

śuddhavidyā Pure knowledge; the intrinsic power of Sadāśiva.

Sugata Another name for Lord Buddha.

Śukrācārya Son of the sage Bhṛgu, one of the seven primordial sages and the teacher of demons; sometimes also called Śukra.

Śuṅga A Buddhist philosopher, expert logician.

śūnya Void; in Buddhism, the highest reality.

śunyavāda The doctrine that advocates that reality is the void or that the void is the highest reality.

Sūrya The sun; also the son of sage Kaśyapa.

Suśena The king who performed the horse sacrifice.

susupti The state of deep sleep.

svātantrya śakti The pure and sovereign power of the highest truth.

tamas The force of nature that is characterized by darkness, heaviness, and inertia.

tantra A spiritual path that provides systematic discipline and practical instruction on the usage of yantra, mantra, meditation, and external rituals.

tattva jñāna The knowledge through which one distinguishes the real from the unreal, *puruṣa* from *prakṛti.*

tattvas Principles or elements; according to Sāṅkhya there are twenty-four, and according to Śaktism there are thirty-six.

Tripurā The Divine Mother; one who pervades and permeates the triple world—waking, dreaming, deep sleep—and the physical, subtle, and causal bodies. Śrīvidyā is another name for Tripurā.

turīya The fourth state of consciousness.

unmanī The state beyond the mind.

upanayana saṁskāra A sacrament; a type of initiation in which a student receives instruction in the practice of the *gāyātrī* mantra, as well as a sacred thread, which he has to wear all the time.

upāsanā Literally, "to come close" to worship.

Vaikuṇṭha The immortal plane attained by great yogis; the abode of Lord Viṣṇu.

vairāgya Non-attachment, dispassion.

Vaiṣṇaivism The philosophy that considers Lord Viṣṇu to be the highest truth.

Vāmadeva One of the famous sages from Vedic and Paurāṇic lore.

Varuṇa The presiding deity of water.

vāsanā Subtle impression of actions which colors the mind.

Vasiṣṭha One of the seven primordial sages.

Vāsudeva Another name for Viṣṇu or Kṛṣṇa.

vata The air element; the force of activity.

Veda Revealed scriptures.

Vicāra Positive thinking; positivity; contemplative awareness; the Vedantic method of *sādhanā.*

Videha One who has transcended body-consciousness; another name for King Janaka.

vidyā Knowledge; wisdom.

Vidyānagara The city of knowledge.

vikalpa Thought constructs; doubts; options.

Viṣṇu The all-pervading God of protection and nourishment.

Viśvakarmā The celestial architect.

Viśvāmitra A famous sage who through his *tapas* became a *brahma ṛṣi;* the seer of the *gāyātrī* mantra and one of the teachers of Lord Rāma.

Vyāsa The sage renowned for his authorship of the voluminous writings called the Pūraṇas.

yakṣa A non-human; a celestial being who is almost equal to the *devas.*

yantra A geometrical figure used as the locus for worshiping tantric deities or for meditation in tantric practices.

yogi One who is adept in the practice of yoga.

ABOUT THE AUTHOR

Pandit Rajmani Tigunait, PhD, is the spiritual head of the Himalayan Institute. Family tradition gave him access to a vast range of spiritual wisdom preserved in both the written and oral traditions. As a young man, he lived and studied with renowned adepts before meeting his spiritual master, Sri Swami Rama of the Himalayas. Pandit Tigunait is fluent in both Vedic and Classical Sanskrit and has an encyclopedic knowledge of the scriptures. He holds a doctorate in Sanskrit from the University of Allahabad, and another in Oriental Studies from the University of Pennsylvania. He has written more than a dozen books, running the gamut from scholarly analysis and scripture translation to spiritual biographies and practical advice on applying yogic concepts to the problems of daily life. In addition to lecturing and teaching worldwide for more than thirty years, Pandit Tigunait is the inspiration for the Institute's rural empowerment projects and the motive force behind the Himalayan Institute Community Centers taking root in Asia and Africa.

THE HIMALAYAN INSTITUTE

The main building of the Institute headquarters near Honesdale, Pennsylvania.

The Himalayan Institute offers educational programs, services, and tools for yoga, meditation, spiritual development, and holistic health. The Institute's mission is spirituality in action, and includes a range of global humanitarian projects in addition to its educational activities. Founded in 1971 by Swami Rama of the Himalayas, the Institute draws on its roots in the ancient tradition of the Himalayan masters to facilitate personal growth and development and service to humanity.

Our international headquarters is located on a beautiful 400-acre campus in the rolling hills of the Pocono Mountains of northeastern Pennsylvania. Our spiritually vibrant community and peaceful setting provide the perfect atmosphere for seminars and retreats, residential programs, and holistic health services. Students from all over the world join us to attend diverse programs on subjects such as hatha yoga, meditation, stress reduction, ayurveda, tantra yoga, and yoga philosophy.

The Institute's global humanitarian projects stimulate transformation and social regeneration through a community center model which provides education, health care, and vocational training. As in all of our work, our approach to humanitarian projects is holistic, multidisciplinary, and spiritually grounded.

Programs and Services Include:

- Himalayan Institute Press
- *Yoga + Joyful Living* magazine
- Seminars and Workshops
- Meditation Retreats
- Yoga Teacher Training
- Self-Transformation Program™
- Residential Programs
- Pancha Karma
- Total Health Center and Products
- Spiritual Excursions
- Humanitarian Projects and Community Centers in Africa and India

We invite you to join us. For further information about our programs or humanitarian activities, or to become a member, call 800-822-4547 or 570-253-5551, write to the Himalayan Institute, 952 Bethany Turnpike, Honesdale, PA, 18431, USA, or visit our website at www.HimalayanInstitute.org.

HIMALAYAN INSTITUTE®
PRESS

The Himalayan Institute Press has long been regarded as the resource for holistic living. We publish books, CDs and DVDs that offer practical methods for living harmoniously and achieving inner balance. Our approach addresses the whole person—body, mind and spirit—integrating the latest scientific knowledge with ancient healing and self-development techniques. As such, we offer a wide array of titles on physical and psychological health and well-being, spiritual growth through meditation and other yogic practices, as well as translations of yogic scriptures.

Our yoga accessories include the *Chakras: Purifying the Subtle Body* packet for meditation practice and the Neti Pot™, the ideal tool for sinus and allergy sufferers. The Total Health® line of quality herbal extracts is available to enhance balanced health and well-being.

Explore ancient wisdom

Tantra Unveiled

Seducing the Forces of Matter & Spirit

Pandit Rajmani Tigunait, PhD

This powerful book describes authentic tantra, what distinguishes it from other spiritual paths, and how the tantric way combines hatha yoga, meditation, visualization, Ayurvedic and other disciplines. Taking us back to ancient times, Pandit Tigunait shares his experiences with tantric masters and the techniques they taught him. *Tantra Unveiled* is most valuable for those who wish to live the essence of tantra—practicing spirituality while experiencing a rich outer life.

Pandit Tigunait is perhaps the most important teacher of tantra in America today.

—David Frawley, author of *Yoga and Ayurveda*

Paperback, $5\frac{1}{2} \times 8\frac{1}{2}$, 168 pages
$14.95, ISBN 0-89389-158-9, B196

Touched by Fire

Pandit Rajmani Tigunait, PhD

This vivid autobiography of a remarkable spiritual leader—Pandit Rajmani Tigunait, PhD—reveals his experiences and encounters with numerous teachers, sages, and his mentor, the late Swami Rama of the Himalayas. His well-told journey is filled with years of disciplined study and the struggle to master the lessons and skills passed to him. *Touched by Fire* brings Western culture a glimpse of Eastern philosophies in a clear, understandable fashion, and provides numerous photographs showing a part of the world many will never see for themselves.

Paperback with flaps, $5\frac{1}{2} \times 8\frac{1}{2}$, 296 pages
$16.50, ISBN 0-89389-239-4, B216GNBH

for ORDERS OR A FREE CATALOG OF BOOKS AND TOOLS FOR YOGA, MEDITATION, AND HEALTH

Call: 800-822-4547 or 570-253-5551 Visit: **www.HimalayanInstitute.org**
Email: mailorder@HimalayanInstitute.org
Write: Himalayan Institute Press, 952 Bethany Tpke, Honesdale, PA 18431

HIMALAYAN INSTITUTE® PRESS

080932